ECONOMIES OF THE EASTERN MEDITERRANEAN REGION

ECONOMIC MIRACLES IN THE MAKING

LEO PAUL DANA, BA, MBA, PhD

Senior Advisor
World Association for Small & Medium Enterprises
&
University of Canterbury, New Zealand

World Scientific

Singapore • New Jersey • London • Hong Kong

Published by

World Scientific Publishing Co. Pte. Ltd.

P O Box 128, Farrer Road, Singapore 912805

USA office: Suite 1B, 1060 Main Street, River Edge, NJ 07661

UK office: 57 Shelton Street, Covent Garden, London WC2H 9HE

British Library Cataloguing-in-Publication Data
A catalogue record for this book is available from the British Library.

ISBN 981-02-4474-6

Printed in Singapore by FuIsland Offset Printing

Dedicated to Ima, Perto and Teresa

Foreword

There was a time, and not too long ago, when consumers in the developed, Western economies associated anything "Made in Japan" with inferior quality and poor value for money. In the 1950s and 1960s, there was no prospect of a country like Japan developing its economic base to such an extent that it could challenge the growing hegemony of the US multinationals. Well, Japan has done this very thing and so too have some of the other Asian tiger economies such as Singapore, South Korea and Malaysia. Indeed, the rate of expansion in some of these economies turned out to be too fast for their own good and hence the recent Asian Crisis.

The important issue being addressed here by Leo Paul Dana concerns the sources of economic development in the first decades of the new millennium. His central thesis, one that is difficult to dispute, is that future development will occur fastest in countries that are in a position to harness three key resources: energy, both mineral and solar; skilled and educated labour available at relatively low cost; and sustained access to knowledge technologies. Rising energy and labour costs in the years ahead will steadily militate against sustained rapid growth in its traditional locations such as North America and the Far East. Dr. Dana makes a powerful case for considering the economies of the Eastern Mediterranean as the locus of the next round of development.

His selection of these countries and his respectful treatment, of each of them, displays the care and professionalism that he has brought to his studies of international entrepreneurship and development. A focus on these countries is indeed rare in the mainstream Western literature. Try looking up Lebanon or Syria in the index of any current international business text! If they are mentioned at all it is likely to be about the difficulty of operating in their distinctive cultures. But their case is made here.

Along the Eastern Mediterranean, one finds energy resources, along with an abundant supply of skilled and affordable labour. An emerging middle class is boosting consumer demand, and the most recent focus is on technological innovation, contributing to the ongoing knowledge revolution. The flow of foreign direct investment into this region in recent years bears testimony to the potential of the area.

Leo Paul Dana is an academic entrepreneur who brings great energy and insight to his work. In this important new book he familiarises us with a region of the world that looks set to play an increasingly prominent part in all of our futures.

Robert T. Hamilton
Faculty Dean
Professor of Management
University of Canterbury, New Zealand

Contents

Preface

Some time ago, while Deputy Director of the International Business MBA Programme of Nanyang Business School, I embarked on the mission to write a book about enterprise along the eastern seaboard of Asia, *i.e.* Pacific Asia. Published in 1999, the book was entitled *Entrepreneurship in Pacific Asia: Past, Present & Future.* In that book, I explained that the concept of Asia originates from the ancient civilisation of Mesopotamia and the eastern shores of the Mediterranean Sea. I mentioned ancient Greek entrepreneurs and Phoenician merchants. As the Greeks cultivated relations with Asians, international trade expanded considerably.

For centuries, the Eastern Mediterranean was the base of the Phoenician trading empire. The Phoenicians were a dominant entrepreneurial culture; they prospered in business, travelling along the Eastern Mediterranean and selling a variety of goods, including clothing and blue glass.

This was the middle of civilisation – hence the name Mediterranean, literally meaning the centre of the world. The shores of the Eastern Mediterranean being on the cross-roads of three continents, the Persians, the Babylonians, the Egyptians, the Greeks and the Romans yearned to control commerce in this wealthy region.

During Roman times, important emirates prospered in this region, although in conflict with the Romans. Among these emirates was Palmyra, which thrived with convoys of silk and spice traders transiting between Rome and the Far East, via the Silk Road.

The concept of an alphabet originated on the shores of the Eastern Mediterranean. Arabic, Greek, Hebrew and Latin scripts are all derived from the first alphabet, devised by mercantile people along the Levant coast.

Although war, politics and economic boycotts delayed the modern development of Mediterranean economies, the recent peace process has given rise to a new era, with innovative concepts and unprecedented opportunities. Not long ago, Israel and Jordan spent large amounts on defence. Today, efforts are focused on economic co-operation.

An innovative creation, in 1998, was the concept of Qualifying Industrial Zones; these offer special treatment to joint ventures that include Israelis and Jordanians working together.

Israel's state-of-the-art technological advances, coupled with low wages among its neighbours, permits cost-efficient production of high quality products, at competitive prices. This is bound to raise the standard of living of all those involved.

The Eastern Mediterranean is rich in talent, technology, and energy. Yet, few Westerners understand the potential of this region at peace. It is once again becoming an important cross-road.

The lands along the eastern shores of the Mediterranean Sea are welcoming foreign investment. Egypt has committed itself to a real growth rate greater than its population growth.

This is a region in which unprecedented opportunities are arising. The region is also home to fascinating cultures, and for most Westerners, it has yet to be discovered. As was said by Benjamin Disraeli, Prime Minister of England, the East is a career.

I was therefore delighted when Commissioning Editor David Sharp suggested to me to write a book about this part of the world. So, here it is.

Leo Paul Dana, BA, MBA, PhD

Acknowledgements

This book could not have been written without field research in the Middle East, and I would like to express gratitude to Delta Airlines, El Al Israel Airlines, Northwest Airlines, and Trans World Airlines for providing complimentary transportation. In addition, airline tickets to Egypt, Greece, Israel and Jordan were provided by Nanyang Business School, of Singapore. The University of Pittsburgh provided transportation to Cyprus, Egypt, and Greece. I would like to thank the Embassy of Egypt in Singapore, for waiving the visa requirement.

© 2000 by Leo Paul Dana

The Author with Assistants

Attendant in Cairo

Acknowledgements   xvii

A special thanks goes to several experts who read and reread chapters, verified facts for accuracy, and provided feedback and suggestions:

- Kholoud Al-Khaldi, Enterprise Development Specialist, in Amman, Jordan
- Anna Anastassopoulou, of McGill University, in Montreal, Canada
- Professor Elena Antonacopoulou, of Manchester Business School, in Manchester, England
- Lina Balawan, of the United Nations Development Programme in the Syrian Arab Republic, in Damascus, Syria
- Ahmed Benani, of the International Observatory for Palestinian Affairs, in Geneva, Switzerland
- Professeur Jean-François Clement, of the Institut Commercial de Nancy Graduate School of Management, in Nancy, France
- Professor Steve Cook, of the Department of Geography at Oregon State University, in Corvallis, Oregon, USA
- Professor Teresa E. Dana, of Nanyang Business School, in Singapore
- Professor Hamid Etemad, of the Faculty of Management at McGill University, in Montreal, Canada
- Professor Ashraf Gamal, of Cairo University, in Cairo, Egypt
- Martyn Henry, editor of *Cyprus Weekly*
- Noga Kadman, of B'Tselem, the Israeli Information Centre for Human Rights in the Occupied Territories
- Heather Lang, of B'Tselem, the Israeli Information Centre for Human Rights in the Occupied Territories
- Androulla Lanitis, of the Ministry of Interior, Government of the Republic of Cyprus
- Professor Sang M. Lee, University Eminent Scholar and Chair, at the Department of Management of the University of Nebraska-Lincoln, in Lincoln, Nebraska, USA
- Professor Yehoshua Lieberman, of Bar Ilan University, in Ramat Gan, Israel
- Canan Ozturan, of the Small and Medium Industry Development Organisation, Turkey
- Professor Michael Perry, of Haifa University, in Haifa, Israel
- Nihaya Qawasmi, of the City University of New York, in New York, USA

- Professeur Loïc Sadoulet, of the INSEAD Asian Campus, in Singapore
- Fernand Sanan, Director of the Centre d'Etudes Bancaires, in Beirut, Lebanon
- Dr. Herbert Leo Scharf, formerly at Harvard Law School, Harvard University, in Cambridge, Massachusetts, USA
- Professor Frederick C. Scherr, of West Virginia University, in Morgantown, West Virginia, USA
- Omar Shaban, of the United Nations Relief & Works Agency, in Gaza
- Professor David Soberman, of INSEAD, in Fontainebleau, France
- Ioannis Solomou, of the Ministry of Interior, Government of the Republic of Cyprus
- Dr. Nabeel Sukkar, Syrian Expert in Economics, in Damascus, Syria
- Professor William P. Thayer, of the Department of History at the University of Kansas, USA
- Professor Behlul Usdiken, of Sabanci University, in Istanbul, Turkey
- Professor Louis Wells, of Harvard Business School, Harvard University, in Cambridge, Massachusetts, USA
- Professor Glen Withiam, of Cornell University, in Ithaca, New York, USA
- Mahmut E. Yalcin, Deputy President of the Small and Medium Industry Development Organisation, in Turkey
- Professor Tela Zaslov, of the University of Pittsburgh Semester-at-Sea Programme, USA

Chapter 1

The Dawn of a New Era

*All animals, except man, know that the
principal business of life is to enjoy it.*
 –   Samuel Butler 1835-1902

History has shown that wartime adversaries – such as Japan and the United
States – and long-time enemies – including France and Germany – can
become heavily interdependent trading partners during times of peace. In the
Middle East, peace is already bringing together former rivals. Four hundred
Egyptians recently returned to Egypt from a training course in Israel, where
they learned to develop the agro-business sector.   The Internet provider
Taskman.com Incorporated is a joint venture bringing Israeli technology to
Jordan; the firm's R & D is conducted in Israel, while a service centre in
Jordan benefits from low wages in that country.

Research suggests that peace in the Middle East shall soon lead to
unprecedented growth and prosperity in the area. The region is on its way to
becoming a great economic power in the global economy.

Take a moment and think about what fuels an economy. Economic
power is largely enhanced by technology, energy, and access to affordable
wages. All these are abundant along the eastern shores of the Mediterranean.

During the late 20th century, Israel emerged as a world-class
technology powerhouse. With a per capita GDP comparable to that in
western European economies, Israel's economy grew at the speed of Asian
tiger economies.

Israel harnessed solar energy and Egypt developed its petroleum
industry. Yet, the lack of peace made it necessary to allocate tremendous
resources to defence concerns. Furthermore, political considerations and a
trade boycott limited the economic potential of the region.

Peace along the Eastern Mediterranean is bound to cause significant change, and countless business opportunities are already arising. Since fighting stopped in Yugoslavia, Greece has become a service provider to its Balkan neighbours, and Greek enterprises are thriving as they contribute to regional development. Albania leaped from a long era of economic backwardness to one of rapid change. Lebanese entrepreneurs are quickly rebuilding their country, which was ravaged during a long civil war; Beirut is becoming an important business centre. Gaza, formerly in occupied territory, now boasts a most modern airport. Cyprus, divided during invasion, is on the brink of joining the European Union. Greek Cypriot entrepreneurs are having exchanges with Turkish Cypriots, who live in the north of Cyprus. Meanwhile, Turkish enterprises from mainland Turkey are prospering in the Turkic-speaking republics of central Asia, including Tajikistan. Technology is spreading, new sources of energy are being developed, and there is an abundance of skilled labour willing to work for relatively low wages. The gap between the Far East and the Middle East is narrowing, as the latter prepares for rapid development. Nations of the former are losing their competitive edge over those of the Eastern Mediterranean.

To understand business today, it is most useful to look at the historical, cultural and social context of enterprise. This is especially so where personal relationships are paramount to success. Characteristic of the Middle East region is the bazaar economy, the subject of Chapter 3. Many people come to the bazaar to sell, or to buy. Others come to socialise and to cultivate personal relationships, not necessarily for any immediate monetary gain.

The eastern shores of the Mediterranean were under Ottoman rule and the influence of Islam can still be noticed here – even in lands that are today predominantly Christian. In this book, constant reference shall be made to historical events, culture and religion, as these are shaping the future.

A reminder of the early days of Islam is the privileged social status accorded to self-employed merchants and artisans. This is not surprising, given the environment in which Islam developed. Mohammed was personally impressed by the camel caravan voyages of traders and on several occasions, in his youth, he travelled with them.

The bazaar is still inter-linked with Islam. During the fasting month of Ramadan, a question that often arises is, "Are you fasting?" During negotiations, there are frequent references to religion. Although Muslims are often secular, it is common to mention Allah during leisure conversation, during business negotiations and even in simple greetings.

Tradition dictates that Muslims should pray five times a day: before sunrise, at noon, during the mid-afternoon, at sunset and at dusk. As traders bargain vividly, behind their voices one can often hear muezzins calling people to pray, from the minarets (of mosques), which serve as public address systems. This custom stems from Bilal, Mohammed's black companion, who called followers to prayer in Medina.

When examining the social structure of the bazaar economy, the relations among the players within it, their organisation and their economic principles, it is useful to consider the power structure involved. In Islam, religion and law are one. Traditionally, the leader of an Islamic community exercises three political powers: executive, legislative and judiciary; in addition, he is considered a religious leader.

The early khalifes, including Omar, Othman and Ali, were considered to be successors to Mohammed, prophet of God. They were regents, judges, military chiefs and religious leaders all in one. According to Ibn Khaldoun, the political and religious leader has the responsibility to protect the religion as well as the direction of the people. Interestingly, such principles survived into the present century.

More striking is the fact that principles of bazaar economics have survived, and these dominate business transactions, often unconsciously. Business in the bazaar economy has traditionally focused on people, relationships and networks. This is in sharp contrast with the firm-type economy of the Occident, where focus has been on the product, rather than on the individual selling it. In the West, economic transactions have tended to be impersonal.

In recent years, however, business in the West has been evolving such that relationship marketing has been gaining importance. Formerly rival firms have been forming alliances, and conducting business as networks. Not long ago, Air Canada and United Airlines competed with Air New Zealand. More recently, membership in the Star Alliance has made them partners in a network of firms. Relationships have become increasingly important. Yet, relationships are even more central in the bazaar, where focus is on a most personal level.

Although networking and other characteristics of the bazaar decreased transaction costs and contributed to efficiency, the countries along the eastern shores of the Mediterranean developed at their own pace – Albania due to political reasons, and other countries due to war and other constraints. Peace in the region is about to signal the dawn of a new era.

Chapter 2

Research Methodology

Man shall have nothing but what he strives for.
– The Qur-an 53:39

This book is the result of primary research conducted by the author. Interviews were conducted with entrepreneurs, corporate executives and government representatives, to provide an insight into the conditions for enterprise in different countries of the Eastern Mediterranean region. Respondents were asked to discuss infrastructure, incentives, opportunities and constraints. As well, documents were consulted to verify details and to obtain additional information.

In Albania, the author interviewed officials at the Ministry of Agriculture; the Ministry of Economic Collaboration & Trade; the Ministry of Foreign Affairs; the Ministry of Information; the Ministry of Labour & Social Affairs; and the Ministry of Public Economy & Privatisation.

In Cyprus, information was obtained from the Civil Aviation Department; the Cyprus Fulbright Commission; the Cyprus Tourism Organisation; the Larnaca Chamber of Commerce; the Ministry of Agriculture, Natural Resources & Environment; the Ministry of Commerce, Industry & Tourism; the Ministry of Finance; and the Ministry of the Interior.

In Egypt, the following were useful sources of information: *Banque du Caire et de Paris*, Garden City; Cairo Far East Bank, Dokki, Giza; Central Bank of Egypt, 31 Kasr El Nil Street, Cairo; Egyptian Export Promotion Centre, Mohandessin, Giza; Federation of Egyptian Industries, 26a Sherif Street, Immobilia Building, Cairo; the General Authority for Investment and Free Zones, 8 Adly Street, Cairo; the Ministry of Agriculture, Animal, Fish Wealth & Land Reclamation, Dokki, Giza; the Ministry of Economy, 8 Adly Street, Cairo; the Ministry of Finance, 1 Maglis el-Shaab Street, Cairo; the Ministry of Industry, Garden City; the Ministry of International Co-operation, Opera Square, Cairo; and the Ministry of Public Enterprises, Garden City.

In Greece, the author was hosted by EOMMEX, the Hellenic Organisation for Medium & Small-Size Enterprises & Handicrafts. Also helpful were the Ministry of Industry, Research Technology and Trade; the Ministry of National Economy; and ELKEPA, the Greek Productivity Centre.

In Israel, the following were most co-operative: Bank Leumi; the Graduate School of Business Administration at Bar Ilan University; the Israel School of Entrepreneurial Management & Innovation; the Ministry of Industry & Trade, 30 Agron Street, Jerusalem; and the Small Business Authority of Israel.

In Jordan, the following provided useful information: the Amman Chamber of Industry; the Central Bank; the Ministry of Finance; the Ministry of Industry & Trade; the Ministry of Planning; the Ministry of Tourism; the Ministry of Transport; Noor A-Hussein Foundation; and the Union of Jordanian Chambers of Commerce.

The chapter about Lebanon was made possible through the co-operation of the Association of Lebanese Industrialists; the *Banque du Liban*; the Chamber of Commerce & Industry of Beirut; the Council for Development & Reconstruction; the Investment Development Authority of Lebanon; the Ministry of Economy & Trade; and the Ministry of Finance.

The Palestinian Authority was very helpful, in particular the Ministry of Economy & Trade; the Ministry of Industry; the Ministry of Interior; and the Ministry of Social Affairs. The Bank of Palestine and the Fishing Association of Gaza were also co-operative. In Gaza, the author was the guest of Omar Shaban, of UNRWA; for details, see the *Alayam* newspaper of Ramallah, May 11 & May 18, 1999.

The chapter about Syria was enhanced by information obtained from the Ministry of Agriculture and Agrarian Reform; the Ministry of Electricity; the Ministry of Finance; Ministry of Foreign Affairs; the Ministry of Industry; the Ministry of the Interior; the Ministry of Irrigation; the Ministry of Social Affairs and Labour; the Ministry of Supply and Internal Trade; and the Office of the Prime Minister. In addition, the United Nations Development Programme in the Syrian Arab Republic was most co-operative.

In Turkey, the following provided the most useful information: KOSGEB (the Small and Medium Industry Development Organisation); MEKSA (the Foundation for Promotion of Vocational Training and Small Industry); TOBB (the Union of Chambers of Industry and Commerce); TOSYÖV (the Turkish Foundation for Small and Medium Enterprises); and TSEK (the Confederation of Turkish Small Scale Industry and Handicrafts).

The Author in Turkey

In Northern Cyprus, the following were most informative: the Chamber of Commerce; the Chamber of Industry; the Department of Immigration; the Department of the Official Receiver & Registrar; the Department of Trade; the Ministry of Economy and & Finance; the Ministry of Foreign Affairs & Defence; and the Ministry of Labour and Social Security.

Chapter 3

The Bazaar Economy*

An American population expert ...called on King Abdul Azziz al Saud, who told him: "You're wasting your time. There are 7 million people here." With apologies, the American said there could not be more than 3 million. "You're wrong," said the King. "There are at least 6 million."...the American insisted...no more than 4 million. At this point the King held out his hand ... bazaar-style, saying "All right, five and a half."
– Time Magazine, May 22, 1978, p.26

Introduction

In Western economies, culture and circumstance have changed the nature of the marketplace. In many places, traditional systems were phased out and replaced by government and/or free-market forces. Western firms are more concerned with market share than with individual buyers.

In contrast, in certain stable economies – such as those along the eastern seaboard of the Mediterranean – cultural values continue to emphasise personal relations, and so the bazaar continues to thrive. Here, people believe that destiny determines who gets a particular sale. An individual will sell, *insha'Allah* – if God wants. Superstition is important and garlic is used to ward off that which is called the evil eye. The survival of the bazaar appears to be linked to the importance of cultural beliefs and personal relationships in a culture. Understanding its dynamics is a prerequisite to succeeding in it.

---

* This chapter was co-authored by Leo Paul Dana and Hamid Etemad, former Associate Dean, McGill University, Montreal, Canada.

Along the Way to the Bazaar

Definitions

The West is familiar with the ***firm-type economy*** – an economic institution, which involves a mode of commercial activity such that industry and trade take place primarily within a set of *impersonally-defined* institutions, grouping people according to organisation and specialisation. It is assumed that profit-maximising transactions will occur based on rational decision-making, rather than on the nature of personal relationships between entrepreneurs and consumers. *The focus is on impersonal transactions.* The decision space is occupied by product attributes and by services attached to them, backed by formal warranties. As a result, the buyer and the individual salesman are secondary, if not trivial, to the transaction decision. The interaction between the buyer and the product (and/or service) is deemed to be more important than that between the buyer and the seller. Competition takes place among sellers. These may be spread across town; they are seldom all in the same district. Segmentation refers to the market. Vendors decide the selling price of a product; this may reflect market forces, including the number of competitors and the price charged by competing firms. Items available for sale are tagged such as to identify the price requested by the vendor.

In contrast, the eastern shores of the Mediterranean are home to the bazaar (*souq*, in Arabic and in Hebrew). The ***bazaar economy*** is a social and cultural system, a way of life and a general mode of commercial activity such that most of the flow of commerce is fragmented into numerous transactions centred on *individuals and personal relationships.* Here, the focus is not on impersonal transactions, but rather on individuals and their inter-relationships. The multiplicity of related small-scale transactions yields an extensive fractionalisation of risks and of profit margins. The bazaar involves production as well as distribution. Furthermore, there are infinite short-term opportunities for small-scale speculation. Yet, complex bookkeeping and managerial accounting are lacking. Nevertheless, space, time, production and sales must be well managed, and personal inter-relations must be managed even more delicately. The units of interest are the entrepreneur, his micro-enterprise and his client. This establishes a personal relationship between buyer and seller. Personal conversations precede an economic transaction. Producers are segmented, often clustered on a street named after them, *e.g.* Bakers Street, Changers' Alley, Fishermen's Wharf, Potato Market, Workman Street, *rue des Bouchers*, etc. Prices are negotiated, as determined by the economically-oriented tension between buyers and sellers. Given the difficulty in determining the value of a product, a sliding price system results in a price within the prevailing limits. Not to negotiate would be seen as a cold-blooded and uncaring avoidance of human contact. Interaction tends to take place between the buyer and the seller, rather than between the buyer and the product. This is summarised in Table 3.1.

BAZAAR ECONOMY	FIRM-TYPE ECONOMY
Focus on personal relations	Focus on impersonal transactions
Segmentation refers to producers	Segmentation refers to the market
Competition refers to tension between buyer and seller	Competition is an activity which takes place between sellers
Prices are negotiated	Prices are indicated

Table 3.1 Economic Systems

How Much Do You Want to Pay?

Ritually-Slaughtered Meat in Fez

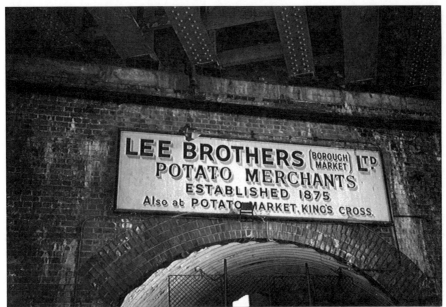

© 2000 by Leo Paul Dana

Potato Merchants in London, England

Historical Overview

Bazaars evolved and thrived in transport-hub cities, such as Kermaan and
Isphahan in Iran, Damascus in Syria and Istanbul in Turkey. Many were
located on ancient trade routes connecting Europe to the Chinese Empire,
through the Persian Empire and the Indian sub-continent. Others served as
nodes along the Sahara Desert.

The southern Silk Road started from Xian, the capital of the Middle
Kingdom (currently in China). With loads of silk and other exotic Chinese
products – including gunpowder, the compass, ink, paper and writing
instruments – caravans headed out to conduct international trade. Indian
spices, as well as Chinese commodities, were traded along the journey.

Also profitable was the trade of finely woven fabrics and carpets in
Kermaan (currently in south-eastern Iran) and expertly-designed jewellery,
ornaments, ceramics and glass works in Isphahan, the capital of the Safavid
dynasty in Iran.

Camels by the Mediterranean

Popular routes passed through population centres, while avoiding mountains and deserts as well as road hazards such as organised bandits. An alternate route travelled through the Central Asian Plateau passing along the shores of the Caspian Sea, toward Asia Minor.

Grand bazaars were critically vital to the functioning of trading routes – including the Silk Road; bazaars formed an infrastructure resembling the hub-and-spoke system of today's air transportation industry. In some ways, the ancient trading caravans were similar to modern airlines: their working capital was relatively large and they were pressed for time. Grand bazaars served as hubs, connected to each other and supplied by caravans travelling the trade routes. Smaller regional bazaars, in neighbouring towns, absorbed some of the imports brought in by caravans, and supplied some of the goods sold to caravans, or bartered. Bazaars thus functioned as inventory depots for the supply chain of other regional bazaars.

In some ways, caravans resembled trade missions of modern times. The most critical aspect of the ancient caravans was time. The long and arduous voyage between Xian and Rome stretched endurance beyond limits. Although the travellers stopped to re-supply along their routes, and rested in organised and strategic locations, called *Caravan-Sara* – literally "home of caravans" in Persian – the traders could not allow disorganised, inefficient, or poor markets to delay their schedule. The ideal bazaars – with a large functional capacity along trade routes – featured the following:

- *Information Dissemination.* Up-to-date supply-related information could be disseminated very fast, due to arbitrage aspects of bazaars.

- *Absorptive Capacity.* The potential buyers and/or their agents (the intermediaries) collectively had sufficient absorptive capacity to make mutually-beneficial spot market transactions with a newly arrived caravan.

- *Supply.* Local suppliers were collectively able to supply caravans with food, drink, inventory and even camels for transport.

- *Efficiency.* The ideal bazaar allowed for the efficient performance of market functions – both, in terms of time, and barter supplies or gold coins, which were available in sufficient supplies only in grand bazaars.

Supplies of Onion at *Sou-el-Bassal*, in Cairo

The bazaar was critical to the continued functioning of international caravan trade; markets enhanced the efficiency of caravans, by acting as clearinghouses. The caravans were thus the predecessors of exporters and export agents, and they manifested many features of today's strategic alliances. In the absence of international law and a modern international trade infrastructure, there was mutual trust and interdependence between traders.

The bazaar agents resembled modern-day importers and import agents, accumulating supplies for normal day-to-day trade, as well as bartering with the caravans. They evidently performed both functions efficiently, and reliably, with mutually respect, to the long-term benefit of all parties.

Hibiscus from Sudan (*Karkade*)

The bazaar imposed discipline. In the absence of large firms and the current facilities of modern corporations, most agents connected to a bazaar had no choice, but to be entrepreneurial. They behaved in ways that we now attribute to creative entrepreneurs, taking and sharing calculated risks, relying on their business network, and acting on opportunity, buying or selling as appropriate.

The supply of foodstuffs was often temporally oriented. The regulating aspect, of the bazaar, balanced supplies over time, such as to satisfy demand throughout the year.

Geographic distance contributed to the disparity between the temporal equilibrium prevailing in each regional market place. This impacted the state of information about overall supplies and demands. The prevailing equilibrium in a market was therefore regional and at times isolated from the overall conditions elsewhere.

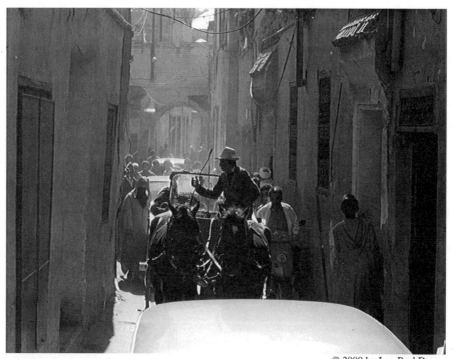

Rush Hour in Marrakech Bazaar

Segmentation by Production

Marketing in the West has led to the sophisticated segmentation of consumers. Firms segment the market and focus on target market segments, consisting of consumers with attributes in common. In contrast, segmentation in the bazaar refers to the geographical clustering of producers, according to the specialisation of suppliers.

The bazaar economy evolved at a time of imperfect markets. Since early market-places were often seasonal, relying on farmers and on their fresh produce, prices reflected supply and demand; they would vary greatly during any given day. In the bazaar, this made possible the efficient clearing of agricultural products, at seasonal markets. From this occasional existence arose the structured market – a stable and permanent structure for buyers and sellers to engage in trading.

© 2000 by Leo Paul Dana

Seasonal Market

Transactions ranged from small, retail sales to very large and complicated wholesale activities. In time, merchants, intermediaries and even customers found efficiency in specialisation, and this led to geographical clustering.

Thus – in contrast to the Occident, where segmentation refers to the market – in the bazaar economy, production is segmented, as are retailers. As early as the 1300s, one of the greatest Arab explorers, namely Ibn Battouta, noted the segmentation of producers and retailers. Even today, shops still are clustered according to the goods offered therein.

Typically, a bazaar might have an area designated for clothing and another for produce; there may be a wing for gold and jewellery, another for carpets, and yet others for spices, fish, etc. Potential buyers and suppliers – of a given good or service – converge on that specific region.

Souq el-Gemal (Camel Market)

High concentration in a given location is critical to efficiency, as it allows for highly efficient information processing. This includes an information search, a comparative evaluation, and decision-making.

In the absence of efficient information processing capabilities, geographically scattered markets would tax operational efficiencies. Finding and then accessing geographically-scattered suppliers – as compared to having them in a concentrated area – would add to transaction costs; an information search through physical access would become more difficult and limited to one's ability.

In contrast to the Occident, where entrepreneurs spread out in order to maximise profit, entrepreneurs in the bazaar prefer to be clustered with others belonging to the same guild, buying from the same supplier and/or selling similar wares. There is little if any differentiation among clustered sellers. In the bazaar, there is considerable co-operation among retailers and among wholesalers. Several entrepreneurs may share a truck, for instance, and there is a sense of belonging to a community. There is a complex balance of carefully managed credit relationships, each with a minute risk.

Guilds (*Al-Sunoof*)

Organisations of employers appeared as early as the ancient Mesopotamian civilisations of Assyria and Babylon. Groups of craftsmen formed associations to safeguard their interests, and to develop relationships, among members as well as between members and the state. To protect their profitability, they created barriers to entry. Simultaneously, they performed a quality control function, by assuring that future members were sufficiently trained by an existing expert. While examining the guild system of the Occident, it is evident that an apprentice in western Europe was dependent on his master and subordinate to him; he was therefore expected to be submissive to the master.

In contrast, in the bazaar economy of the Eastern Mediterranean, the greatest difference between a master and an apprentice is simply professional qualification. While the European guild focused on production, the focus in the bazaar is on pride in one's work and in belonging to a community. Hierarchy in the bazaar is less structured than in the West.

© 2000 by Leo Paul Dana

Master with Apprentice

The guilds of the Eastern Mediterranean bazaars never had as much power as did those in the West. Nevertheless, fees were collected from members, and funds were raised to grant financial assistance to new ventures.

Competition & Pricing

While "competition" in the firm-type economy is understood to take place between sellers, "competition" in the bazaar refers to the tension between buyer and seller, rather than between sellers. The lack of information results in a very imperfect market, and with few exceptions, such as basic food staples, retail prices are not indicated but rather these are determined by negotiations. The customer first tests price levels informally, and only later begins to bargain. Often it is the buyer who proposes a price, which is eventually raised. Once a mutually satisfactory transaction has taken place, it is desirable to establish a long-term relationship. This makes future purchases more pleasurable and efficient, as less time is spent negotiating, and more can be allocated to drinking tea, for instance. Effective communication is essential, allowing a sale to be equated to pleasure, rather than work. Sometimes, a consumer sends his wife to bargain, hoping that gallantry will yield better prices.

Prices are generally firm and high in the morning. By the afternoon, vendors are often less likely to maintain high prices, especially when the effect of heat diminishes one's energy. It is a tradition to give a discount to the last customer of the day. This may be due to the recognition that consumers have a choice and the quality of remaining stock decreases with time. Also, a vendor with remaining inventory, at the end of the day, incurs transportation and possibly storage costs; in the case of perishables, the situation is aggravated. Thus, price is a function of a variety of factors, including cost, perceived value, time, negotiating skills and circumstances.

A Typical Bazaar

A bazaar functions reasonably efficiently, largely thanks to the geographical concentration and clustering of vendors in like occupations. Yet, this is not obvious to the Westerner. A comprehension of the social context of the bazaar is most helpful, when trying to understand the particular way of functioning of the bazaar economy.

The structured bazaar allows physical concentration. This enables potential buyers and suppliers to meet efficiently at a pre-determined location. This reduces search costs and minimises disparity caused by geographic fragmentation. Thus, the bazaar reduces overall transaction costs, as all parties concerned converge on a central location.

In a structured bazaar, one can observe a distinct pattern of economic activity. A potential buyer can easily locate the designated part of the bazaar for goods/services under consideration. Once at that location, it is possible to compare the goods of several dealers, within a short span of time. This allows the shopper to develop a feel for the prevailing market conditions, including the price and supply range. As more supplies enter or exit the market over time, and as the range shifts, the potential buyer can decide when and how to take a definitive position (*i.e.,* to buy or to defer). The structured bazaar provides vital market functions including the following:

- *Information Dissemination.* Individuals disseminate their proprietary information regarding new products and emerging trends in supply or demand.

- *Updating.* Potential suppliers and buyers quickly update and upgrade their state of information and incorporate their new knowledge to assume a new position.

- *Temporal Equilibrium.* Some potential suppliers and buyers behave as intermediaries, and they profit from arbitrage. They engage in co-operative bargaining and negotiations, forming strategic alliances.

- *Control.* The non-committal nature of arbitrage – coupled with the bazaar-imposed sense of ethics – regulates behaviour in the bazaar, and by extension the bazaar itself. Traders are ethically bound to honour their words. The possible enforcement of collective sanctions controls both the frequency and the range of fluctuations in the bazaar.

With little variations, the style and procedures of trade, in the bazaar, reflect a certain pattern:

1) A potential buyer inquires about supplies and prices from *several* suppliers, within eye-and-ear-shot of each other. This allows the person to form a reasonably informed opinion about the state of the market at the time.

2a) When the person's initial intention is to buy, he returns to a dealer and attempts to negotiate the price, by making an offer or counter-offer.

2b) When the initial intention is to sell to a dealer at the bazaar, a person may return to the dealer with the highest selling, to offer a wholesale transaction.

A justification is usually offered through the use of a typical negotiation ploy such as: "Another dealer is selling the same at this price, but I would like to do business with you, because of our past relation." The response may be along the lines of one of three alternatives:

a) To ignore the counter-offer as a ploy based on what he knew of the prevailing tight range of prices and supplies (especially when the offered price is outside or close to the lower bound of the price range);

b) To attempt to unload his supplies with a firm counter-offer of his own by splitting the difference on the price side and conditioning it upon a larger quantity than required by the potential buyer; or

c) To offer to buy a quantity (as opposed to selling) at the offered price, to both impact the dynamics of that transaction and the market by signalling a readiness to sell or buy. This is a sufficiently logical behaviour to influence the decision of potential buyers, regardless of initial intentions.

Bazaar-imposed ethics oblige buyers and sellers to honour their words. This is the foundation of the concept of trust. Two outcomes are common:

- The prospective buyer succeeds to buy at a fair price when the buyer's intention was to buy at close to the prevailing equilibrium price.

- A new price level begins to prevail when arbitrage was the original intention in the above characterisation. The increasing possibility of intermediaries participating in a perceived imbalance in the market place allows for virtual consummation of many transactions at prices associated with total supply and demand at each moment in time.

Ongoing arbitrage – combined and enforced by bazaar-imposed discipline – thus accords the structured bazaar functional efficiency, even in modern times.

Managerial Implications

In the bazaar, personal relations are more important than are impersonal transactions. There is little, if any concern about market share.

To the Western manager, the economics of the bazaar may not be evident. Yet, the bazaar does have its efficiency and along the Eastern Mediterranean entrepreneurs still function with a bazaar mindset. A Westerner who approaches the bazaar, with an understanding of the bazaar belief system, is likely to succeed better than those who assume a Western orientation.

© 2000 by Leo Paul Dana

Delivery Service in the Bazaar

Chapter 4

The Republic of Albania

Introduction

Known to Albanians as *Shiqipëria*, Albania covers 28,752 square kilometres. Its neighbours are the Former Yugoslav Republic of Macedonia, Greece, Kosovo and Montenegro. Albania is rich in oil, natural gas, chromium, copper and other mineral resources. Its people are divided into two dialect groups; Gheg is prevalent in the north and Tosk (the official dialect) in the south. Many Albanians speak Italian, German, Russian, English and/or French.

After several decades of centralised planning, and a policy of isolationism, Albania was described by the Bretton Woods institutions as being among the most successful transforming countries of Eastern Europe. The European Union ranked Albania the highest, among post-communist nations in overall satisfaction with economic reforms.

Historical Overview

In Roman times, the land currently known as Albania was part of the provinces of Epirus and Illyria. When the Roman Empire was split during the 4th century, the territory was assigned to the Byzantine Empire. Then came invasions by Goths and Slavs. During the 9th century, Bulgaria absorbed Albania.

The Albanians first became independent during the 15th century, under a Gheg known as Gjergi Kastrioti Skanderbeg. Independence did not last long, as the country soon fell under Ottoman rule, which lasted until 1912 when Albania became a principality under Prince William of Wied.

Traditional Albanian with Her Flock

A president was named in 1925, and in 1928 he became King Zog I. During his rule, a trade agreement with Italy encouraged foreign investment, but illiteracy in Albania was still 85%.

In 1939 Benito Mussolini seized control of Albania, and the country was occupied by the Italians. The Nazis arrived, in 1943, asking for a list of Jews, but the government refused to co-operate. The Albanian resistance announced that anyone refusing to give sanctuary to Jews would be subject to execution, "for the crime of dishonouring the Albanian people." Thus, the entire community escaped the Holocaust. Nazi occupation ended in 1944.

When the Albanian People's Republic was proclaimed, the country became communist, under the totalitarian rule of Enver Hoxha, perhaps the most eccentric dictator in Eastern Europe. He banned bananas, beards, bright colours, foreign journalists, most imports, and even religion. Hoxha denounced the communist parties of Yugoslavia (in 1948), of the USSR (in 1961), and of China (in 1978). Paranoid of invasion, he built concrete bunkers across the country.

© 2000 by Leo Paul Dana

One of Countless Bunkers Across Albania

Introducing Free Enterprise

After the death of Hoxha in 1985, Ramiz Alia became president, and slowly led the way to *Perseritje*, the Albanian version of *Perestroika*. Dana (1996) discusses the *Perseritje* Model at length.

President Alia proposed more scope for small business and introduced some liberal reforms. Yet, in 1987, there were only forty automobiles in Albania. As the 1990s approached, main streets in the capital city still looked liked country lanes, with trucks but few cars.

Trucks Had Been Imported from China

Alia was swept from power during Albania's first post-communist elections in 1992, when Sali Berisha succeeded him. Urban unemployment was about 50% that year.

Recovery began in 1993, and by 1994, the unemployment rate was falling and inflation was reduced to an annual rate of 30%. Self-employment became widespread. In recognition of progress, in 1994 the International Monetary Fund approved a further extended arrangement with Albania.

Self-employed Retailers Prospered When Bananas Were Legalised

Young Vendor in the New Market Economy

By the mid-1990s, output was growing more than 10% a year, and an entrepreneurial mindset was replacing communist ideology. Pages from Hoxha's books were being used to package roasted almonds or sausages.

Using Hoxha's Book to Serve Sausages

Although the collapse of pyramid investment schemes, in 1997, led to a brief crisis, the economic situation stabilised in 1998. In November 1998, a popular referendum endorsed the new constitution. In 1999, 450,000 refugees arrived in Albania, escaping conflict in Kosovo. While the inflow of 20,000 NATO soldiers put an end to rampant crime, journalists and aid workers from 180 different organisations meant good business for hotels and guesthouses. This was an unexpected boost for the Albanian economy.

Renting an Extra Room in Her Home

©2000 by Leo Paul Dana

Albtursit Hotels Were Privatised

©2000 by Leo Paul Dana

In 1999, the Albanian economy grew by at least 8%, while inflation did not exceed 1%. The currency strengthened vis-à-vis the American dollar.

Albanian Currency

Agriculture

In 1992, huge prairie fields of the Albanian agricultural system were privatised. This gave rise to 400,000 self-employed farmers, each with a private strip of land. Over half of Albania's GDP is derived from agricultural activities, a sector employing about half of the working population.

In addition to using their own property, farmers also graze their animals along the roadside. It is common, for example, in 40°C heat, to see a Muslim woman, her head covered, walking her sheep on a rope. Cows, goats and sheep are raised not only for their meat, but also for their milk, cheese and wool. The hides are also an economically important by-product. Poultry are common, not only among farmers; even urbanites often have a few chickens and a rooster by their home. Honey is harvested, and a Riesling wine is locally produced. Agricultural produce includes barley, beans, corn, figs, grapes, honey, lemons, oats, olives, pomegranates, rice, rye, tobacco, tomatoes, and watermelons.

©2000 by Leo Paul Dana

Watermelon Season

Since the privatisation of farmland, Albanian farmers are obtaining intrinsic job satisfaction, previously non-existent. This appears to be motivating them considerably. In contrast to the constant shortages experienced during communist rule, local agricultural products are now plentiful. At the indoor market stalls of Durres, it is possible to purchase a variety of produce, including fresh cantaloupe, eggs, garlic, green peppers, okra, potatoes and watermelon. Peaches are available, either canned or fresh. It is also possible to buy tomatoes, which are grown in local greenhouses. Local and imported wheat is available in abundance. The food shortages of recent years seem to have been forgotten.

Market at the Cross-roads

Changing Values

Under dictatorship, Albania used to barter tomatoes for violins from
Czechoslovakia; Albania had 29 music schools, and Albanian students
would practice several hours a day. Anyone caught listening to Western
music would be sent to forced-labour prison. At the central Tirana music
conservatory, *Misja Artistik Shkola*, an old building with many broken
windows, some students still practice, in damp, dimly-lit corridors. However,
music schools are losing popularity as youths realise that they can earn more
in one day working as a waiter in neighbouring Greece than during many
days as a musician in Albania. American music is no longer prohibited in
Albania.

Religion, banned in 1967, was permitted again in November 1990. The harmony between Muslims and Orthodox Christians is remarkable. While multitudes of people worship at the main mosque in Tirana, and new mosques are being built, many people can be seen wearing crosses in public. Muslim and Orthodox Christian death notices are posted side by side.

Investment

The new mindset, along with privatisation and business-friendly legislation, is contributing to a healthy environment for business. This includes small-scale micro-enterprises, as well as larger new ventures and foreign investment.

© 2000 by Leo Paul Dana

Formerly a State Factory

Impromptu Stall Selling Drinks Along the Railway Tracks

In November 1993, a new and liberal Foreign Investment Law permitted foreign investments, without prior authorisation or licensing requirements. Since then, the law has treated local and foreign investors alike. Capital may exit Albania without difficulty.

The Albanian Economic Development Agency, a joint stock company, was created in August 1998, by the Albanian Government. Its purpose is to encourage and facilitate domestic and foreign investment, in order to stimulate economic growth in Albania. The agency consists of three departments, allowing for the efficient management of several activities: the preparation, publishing and distribution of economic promotional materials (by the Department of Information & Publishing); the identification of opportunities, the promotion of international trade, and the promotion of Albania as an attractive environment for investment, and assistance to investors (by the Department of Promotion and Consultancy); and assistance to the government, in the formulation of promotion policies, strategies, and in reforming the legal framework for investment (by the Department of Personnel, Administration and Finance).

The Albanian Economic Development Agency provides potential investors with details of firms about to be privatised, and it offers consulting services to potential investors. As well, it assists small, local companies wishing to expand or to participate in joint ventures. The agency prepares company profiles and serves as a matchmaker. In addition, it hosts trade fairs, seminars, conferences, and roundtables on various economic issues. It also provides training in business, economic issues and business law.

In accordance with Decision 463 of the Council of Ministers, on October 6, 1999, amended by Decision 123 on March 18, 2000, the Ministry of Public Economy & Privatisation announced the privatisation of four leading enterprises in Albania. These were: Ajka, the largest dairy and producer of cheese and yoghurt in the country; Birra Malto, Albania's largest brewery; Kantina, the nation's largest producer of wines and spirits in Albania; and Proforma, the largest producer of pharmaceuticals.

The four consumer-oriented firms were transformed into joint stock companies, and it was decided that employees be allowed to participate in the privatisation. In the case of Birra Malto, for instance, 6% of the shares were reserved for individuals related to the company, and the remaining 94% were offered to the public.

The Council of Ministers decided to sell each of the above-mentioned businesses by tender, awarding them based on five criteria: (i) the price offered for the shares; (ii) the level of proposed investment; (iii) the business plan and technical quality of the proposal; (iv) the previous achievements of the investor; and (v) the plan for re-training and employment. Each tender required a guarantee deposit of $30,000,[1] blocked in a bank account of the National Agency of Privatisation at the Savings Bank of Albania, in Tirana.

A Bid Evaluation Committee – including representatives from the Ministry of Public Economy and Privatisation, and the National Agency for Privatisation – was responsible for ranking the bidders. The recommendations of the committee would be implemented only if and when approval by the Council of Ministers.

---

[1] Throughout this book, $ refers to US dollars.

The Albanian Guarantee Agency administers the Risks Guarantee Facility, involving World Bank funds, to increase investor confidence in Albania. This programme provides insurance from political risks, war, civil unrest, tax increases, and trade bans.

Toward the Future

Albania is no longer perceived as a source of problems, but as a land of opportunity. The government's attitude, during the 1999 Kosovo Crisis, launched a new image of Albania; since NATO used Albania as a supply base, the international community welcomed Albania as a partner.

Albania's growth-oriented reform programme, based on free market economic principles, law and order, is being implemented with the co-operation of the International Monetary Fund. In March 2000, Albania approached the international donor community in Brussels, with plans to modernise the port at Durres.

© 2000 by Leo Paul Dana

The Port of Durres

Tirana, a quiet town during the author's first visit in 1994, is now bustling with fashionable shoppers, eager to display their newly-acquired spending power. Rising disposable incomes have boosted consumer demand. As well, the service sector – underdeveloped until the 1990s – is booming.

© 2000 by Leo Paul Dana

Discussing the Future

Albania has an abundance of mineral wealth which, if properly exploited, could contribute to exports in the future. For instance, Albania has offshore oil as well as 5% of the world's deposits of chrome-bearing ore. An infrastructure of pipelines is already in place, for crude oil and natural gas.

Private foreign direct investment into Albania has been escalating as investors wish to participate in this rapidly emerging market. The European Commission has approved a feasibility study for Albania's accession into the European Union. Albania's economy is set to grow, during the next few years, at a rate close to 8% per annum.

Chapter 5

The Republic of Cyprus

Introduction

Cyprus is the third largest island in the Mediterranean Sea. The Republic of Cyprus, an industrial and export-oriented nation, with a thriving service sector, is a candidate for membership in the European Union. Greek and Turkish are official languages here, while English is also widely spoken.

Trilingual Sign

Since 1974, the northern part of Cyprus has been occupied by Turkish forces, as will be discussed in Chapter 14. About 180,000 Greek Cypriots were driven out of their homes and became refugees. The boundary between the Republic of Cyprus and the occupied territory is called the Green Line. It cuts through Nicosia – the capital city of both entities – just as the Berlin Wall once did in Germany. Along the cease-fire line, there are houses with broken windows and missing doors. Sandbags are still piled where windowpanes used to be.

© 2000 by Leo Paul Dana

Sandbags at the Green Line

Soldiers, standing tall, on balconies, guarding their posts, are still using their binoculars, as if an ambush were about to happen. At the control post, a cross can be seen leaning against a dilapidated building, a map of Cyprus hung on the posts and a knife jabbed in its heart, where Nicosia lies. Huge billboards prominently display the killing of two Greek Christians. Literature is distributed to inform visitors of such incidents.

On the south side of the Green Line, Greek Cypriot National Guardsmen watch the Turkish Cypriot troops, and others from mainland Turkey, across a narrow street covered in weeds. Just a few metres away, in the heart of town, a Greek Cypriot entrepreneur manages his restaurant. He solicits new clients and makes sandwiches; while his clients are eating, he repairs a window. According to his culture, working hard is good.

Nearby, five ice-cream shops – within a short distance of each other – are evidence of the abundance of disposable income in this country. To be seen spending is desirable in this society. Big brand names are popular and prominently featured. These include the Body Shop, Kodak and McDonald's; KFC is promoting its delivery service.

Seven-Up, Popular Since the British Era

Sophisticated marketing plans from the West, and increased marketing costs, coupled with high local demand, have sustained rising prices. Western influence has also brought sex shops, cabarets and hotels that rent rooms by the hour. At some establishments in Nicosia, it is impossible to rent a room without receiving a woman – or girl – as part of the package and included in the price.

Historical Overview

The strategic location of Cyprus made it a commercial hub for early traders, and, over the years, various powers have wanted to rule it. Fortified walls still remain, as evidence of Venetian rule that lasted until 1571. Then, the Turks conquered the island, and it remained Ottoman until 1878, at which time the British took over its administration. In 1925, Cyprus became a British Colony, with King George V as head of state.

George VI, Head of State 1936-1952

During World War II, Cyprus became a haven for Greek refugees escaping the Nazis on the Aegean Islands. Between 1942 and 1945, about 12,000 Greek refugees were settled in camps provided by the state and the Cyprus Mines Corporation. Most of these refugees settled in Cyprus permanently. There were also Jews who sojourned briefly in Cyprus on their way to British Palestine (see Chapter 8).

During the 1950s, agriculture accounted for 40% of gainful employment in Cyprus. This contributed greatly to exports.

On August 16, 1960, the Republic of Cyprus was formally declared independent from the United Kingdom, and for the first time established its own ruling body. The national constitution was drafted by Britain and endorsed by Greece and by Turkey. Article 185 stipulated that "the territory of the Republic of Cyprus is one and indivisible." The new republic maintained close trading links with England and with other members of the British Commonwealth.

While most of the islanders were Greek Orthodox Christians, a Muslim minority gradually gained significant power. In 1974, Turkey invaded the north of Cyprus, creating a puppet republic. During their invasion, the Turks bombed much of the island's lush forests. Replanting trees has taken time, but the results are now visible over the rolling hills of the south. Foresters patrol these areas, ensuring the success of the projects.

Two Cultures

The name "Cyprus" is believed to be derived from the Latin term for copper – *Cyprium aes* – the principal economic resource on the island. This is reflected in the national flag, which is white, with a copper-coloured silhouette of the entire island. Below the silhouette are two olive branches symbolising the hope for peace between the Greeks and the Turks who make up the island's two ethnic communities.

Eighty percent of the island's population is Greek Orthodox. Most (99.5%) of these people reside in the Republic of Cyprus. The majority of the Muslims (98.7%) reside in the self-proclaimed Turkish Republic of Northern Cyprus, the topic of Chapter 14. The population of the Republic of Cyprus is quite homogeneous, since 95% of the people are Greek Orthodox. During the late 20th century, the national labour force of the Republic of Cyprus approached 300,000 people, 65% of whom worked in services, 25% in industry and 10% in agriculture.

Greek Orthodox Priest in Cyprus

A Macro-Economic Overview

The Republic of Cyprus joined the United Nations in 1960. Since 1961, it has been a member of the British Commonwealth, of the Council of Europe, and of the Non-Aligned Movement. The Association Agreement between Cyprus and the European Economic Community (the predecessor to the European Union) came into effect in 1973. The Republic of Cyprus is a member of the International Monetary Fund and of the World Bank, both of which classify it as a developed nation.

The Cyprus Organisation for Standards and Control of Quality is the national standards body. It is a full member of the International Standards Organisation (ISO), and its activities include preparation and publication of standards, inspection, conformity assessment, and certification.

Given the limited size of the domestic market, an export-orientation is common among Cypriot enterprises. Trade is facilitated by a customs agreement with the European Union.

The Larnaca Free Trade Zone is an industrial estate into which equipment, machinery and materials are brought in without duty. Exports include bathroom equipment, cement, clothes, footwear and precision instruments sold to customers in Germany, Greece, Lebanon, the United Kingdom and Arab states.

The domestic economy is highly diversified. The village of Lefkara is well known for its lace and silverware. Not far, the monastery of Ayios Minas is famous for the production of honey and painting of icons. The monks of the Chrysoroyiatissa Monastery are said to produce some of the island's best vintage wines. However, the agricultural sector is on the decline. Government incentives have precipitated industrialisation; the transformation of the republic into a tax haven has created opportunities in the service industries, while the state created dis-incentives for entrepreneurs in agriculture. The acquisition of farmland and of pastures, in the Republic of Cyprus, is subject to a transfer tax of five to eight percent of its market value. Even transfers between relatives are taxable. The transfer of a farm between spouses is taxed at 8%; from parents to children, the rate is 4%.

Income tax reform, in 1990, favoured entrepreneurs in tertiary industries as opposed to those in agriculture. Regional bus companies became eligible for a 100% accelerated allowance on the cost of new buses acquired after 1984. In addition to this accelerated allowance, an investment allowance of 45% is permitted during the year of acquisition of new vehicles.

© 2000 by Leo Paul Dana

Veteran Bus

Cars and trucks may be depreciated up to 25% each subsequent year. Business equipment, such as computers, software and robots, is eligible for an investment allowance of 40% during the year of purchase. The same is true of machinery used by joint ventures. In contrast, farm machinery is depreciable by a negligible amount. Farmers are eligible for a capital gains tax exemption, only when disposing of agricultural land.

The Customs and Excise Law also encouraged a shift away from agriculture. Food items may be brought into the Republic of Cyprus free of duty. Woollen goods from the British Commonwealth also enter duty-free. Not surprisingly, Cypriot farmers have been selling their fields, and shepherds have been disposing of their flocks. Yet, Cyprus is nevertheless self-sufficient in fruits, vegetables, vines, milk, eggs, poultry, and pork. As well, cereals, olives, cattle, sheep and goats are in abundance.

Free Zone Law 69/1975 provides special treatment to enterprises manufacturing new products in the Republic of Cyprus. Also contributing to the development of the manufacturing sector is the Industrial Training Authority, which provides industrial training in all sectors of industry. Its expenses are covered by a fund into which every employer pays an amount equal to half of 1% of salary disbursements.

Seventy-four percent of gross domestic product in the Republic of Cyprus is derived from services, 11% from manufacturing, 7% from construction and 5% from agriculture. Inflation in this country has followed a downward trend, reaching 1.7% in 1999.

Infrastructure

The Republic of Cyprus has long had an excellent infrastructure. Telecommunications and transportation networks are well developed. There are two international airports, one near Larnaca and the other near Paphos. These are served by 35 scheduled airlines and another 82 charter operators.

The national flag-carrier – Cyprus Airways – has a market share of approximately 26%. In 1999, international air traffic using these airports came to 5,658,851 passengers.

Cyprus has one of the world's largest shipping registries, with over 2,600 ships. Its merchant fleet ranks sixth in the world. About 70 management companies make Cyprus one of the largest third-party ship-management centres. The geographic position of Cyprus, coupled with tax incentives, a highly educated workforce and minimal regulation, contribute to the attractiveness of Cyprus as a trans-shipping hub. While Larnaca and Limassol are multi-purpose ports, there are also specialised oil terminals at Dhekelia and Moni, as well as an industrial port at Vassiliko. About 70 lines serve Cyprus regularly, with an annual 15 million net tonnes registered at Cyprus ports; approximately 4,000 ships dock in Cyprus each year. Transit cargoes benefit from free trade facilities, low-cost long-term storage and minimal paperwork requirements.

Until late 1997, there were only three telephone lines crossing the Green Line. The United Nations controlled the lines, and calls were connected manually, via an operator; connections were made only between 7 a.m. and 10 p.m. In November 1997, Greek Cypriot and Turkish Cypriot entrepreneurs met at conference in Brussels, where both sides expressed interest in improved telecommunication facilities between the two sides. There, it was agreed to expand telephone services such as to include 20 automatic lines, which could be used 24 hours a day. It was estimated, at the time, that 100,000 phone calls would be made yearly. The cost of the system – $150,000 – was borne by the United States. According to the United Nations Peacekeeping Force in Cyprus, 354,647 calls were made across the Green Line in 1999.

Banking

The Republic of Cyprus has long enjoyed a good banking infrastructure, and capital is freely transferable without any exchange control restrictions. The Bank of Cyprus Ltd., which has been in operation since 1899, is the largest commercial bank in the country. The National Bank of Greece has been present here since 1907. The Cyprus Popular Bank Ltd. was created in 1924; the Hong Kong and Shanghai Banking Corporation holds 22.23% of its shares. Accounts may be opened in any of several currencies, and interest income on foreign capital is non-taxable. There is also a very well-developed international banking system.

The Interest Law of 1944 limited interest rates in the Republic of Cyprus. The Interest Law of 1977 set the legal interest rate to 9%.

In 1992, the Cyprus pound (C£), was linked to the ECU, at the rate of 1.7086 ECUs per pound, plus or minus 2.25%. This rate now applies to the Euro.

Recent legislation repealed the Interest Law, effective January 1, 2001. Reform called for greater transparency of credit institutions.

The Legal Environment

Until the 1990s, the law for family matters of Greek Orthodox Cypriots was the common law of the Orthodox Church; according to recent legislation, family law is no longer administered by the church, but rather by the courts. However, in order for divorcees to get remarried in a church, a couple must apply to their bishop to get a religious divorce, in addition to a civil one.

The commercial legal system, in the Republic of Cyprus, closely resembles that in England. Statutory and reporting requirements for incorporated businesses are very similar to those of the Companies Act 1948, of the United Kingdom. Chapter 116 of the legislation specifies that any foreigner is entitled to carry on an enterprise in the Republic of Cyprus.

Income arising outside Cyprus is not taxable. There are no withholding taxes on dividends. Double taxation treaties, with twenty-seven countries, provide relief from foreign taxes. The Republic of Cyprus provides tax-sparing credits allowing entrepreneurs to reduce their tax liabilities overseas, without actually paying tax in Cyprus. Income derived from interest on foreign capital, which is imported and subsequently lent for the purpose of financing approved investments, is tax-exempt for the first five years of activity. The Customs and Excise Law allows entrepreneurs to import office equipment, household effects and motor vehicles free from duty.

In 1975, legislation was enacted to attract, to Cyprus, entrepreneurs who would create International Business Companies.[2] The ceiling on corporation tax payable by International Business Companies is 4.25%. In some cases, employees of these enterprises are entitled to tax-free income.

In 1992, the Republic of Cyprus passed the International Trusts Law, allowing entrepreneurs to trade anonymously, without disclosing the beneficiaries of a business activity. The Insurance Companies Law allows small-scale insurance firms (with as little as C£10,000 in capital) to operate without guarantees or solvency margins. Entrepreneurs may also use the Republic of Cyprus as a letterhead address, for their corporate headquarters, for trading.

---

[2] Cyprus defines an International Business Company as a business registered in Cyprus, operating under Cyprus Law, but whose ownership rests with foreigners, and whose income is derived outside Cyprus.

The legal environment has propelled the number of foreign firms in the republic, from 83 in 1976, to almost 40,000 in 2000. Most do not physically operate on the island; only about 1,000 have a fully-functioning office in the country, while the majority operates overseas. Among these are general traders, builders, engineers, printers, publishers, employment agencies, finance companies, investment consultants, insurance providers and royalty entities.

Tourism

Tourism is the most important economic activity in Cyprus, with Israel being one of the most important source markets. In 1999, 61,029 tourists from Israel visited Cyprus, up 14% from 1998. Receipts from tourism rose to C£1.022 billion in 1999, representing about one fifth of the GNP.

Government policy calls for the development of sustainable tourist packages, promoting local culture, history and tradition. The state encourages private investment in the sector, and growth in the tourism industry is spurring new opportunities for entrepreneurs. New ventures include travel agencies, bed and breakfast operations, hotels, car rental establishments, mini-bus services, restaurants, moneychangers, discotheques and water-sport recreation enterprises. When the Civil Aviation Department decided to expand the Larnaca International Airport, this created opportunities for contractors and sub-contractors.

Toward the Future

The European Union is the main trading partner of the Republic of Cyprus, accounting for over 50% of the latter's trade and 60% of tourist arrivals. The republic has been recommended for membership in the European Union, along with the Czech Republic, Estonia, Hungary, Poland and Slovenia. In November 1997, the Foreign Affairs Committee of the European Parliament adopted a resolution that Turkey cannot block the accession of Cyprus to the European Union. Also in November 1997, entrepreneurs from the north and from the south of Cyprus met in Brussels, to discuss issues of mutual co-operation in the business realm. They decided to create a business forum for north-south contacts and agreed to establish a common courier service for north-south business correspondence.

© 2000 by Leo Paul Dana

The Road to the North is Blocked, but Probably Not for Long

Outside the physical sciences, Cyprus presents a rare opportunity to draw conclusions from that which is almost a controlled in-vitro experiment. The inland was divided into two sectors with comparable natural resources; a different culture and a set of related consequences influenced each. Although the distribution of natural resources was not significantly different, the Republic of Cyprus implemented a pro-enterprise policy, allowing its society to become considerably wealthier than that of its neighbour. The Republic of Cyprus is an important offshore financial and maritime centre, a holiday destination and a commercial hub with growing, export-oriented industries.

Chapter 6

The Arab Republic of Egypt

An achievement that has few parallels.
– The International Monetary Fund

Introduction

Egypt covers just over 1 million square kilometres, spanning from north-eastern Africa into the Sinai Desert, in western Asia. It has a large domestic market and highly productive land, with increasing productivity.

Only a decade ago, Brockhaus observed that "the culture of Egypt is such that a very weak private enterprise system exists except in the informal sector (1991, p.81)." Since then, ambitious structural reforms have drastically transformed Egypt. The role of government has shifted from that of regulator to that of facilitator. Today, Egypt has the largest economy in North Africa and the second largest in the Arab world. It is the largest developer of Arabic software.

Egypt offers an excellent environment for business. Its people provide talented labour at highly competitive wages. Also, the country has an abundance of low-cost materials and inexpensive utilities, in addition to a developed transportation network, including direct access to the Suez Canal as well as major ports on the Mediterranean Sea and on the Red Sea. To further attract investment, the state has introduced Free Zones, as well as Inland Investment Incentives. The Free Zones are home to over 1,000 companies operating on land which is considered beyond the boundaries of Egypt's customs regulations; firms in these zones are exempt from duties and from income tax on profits, as long as their product is exported.

Historical Overview

Located at the junction of Africa and Asia, Egypt has long been a cross-road of trade. The ancient Egyptians were among the world's first great civilisations. These people were already trade-oriented 5,000 years ago. The Great Sphinx – about 75 metres long and 20 metres high – was carved about 4,500 years ago.

The Great Sphinx

The Egyptians were among the first nations in the world to learn to use metals. For thousands of years, men here have worked as metal-smiths, making jewellery, knives, swords and the like.

Records, from about 1500 BC, list cargo boats on the Nile, and describe their freight with meticulous detail. Every nobleman of the time employed a staff of scribes, in charge of accounting. Each goat and pigeon, on an estate, was recorded. It was the ancient Egyptians who invented papyrus – from which the English word "paper" was derived.

During the rule of Pharaoh Ramses II (circa 1240 BC), self-employed artisans in Egypt were making jewellery and small-scale industry included perfume manufacturing. Typical of the bazaar economy, prices were negotiated.

About 2,500 years ago, Egypt developed very good relations with Greece, and Greek traders settled in the Nile River Delta. In 30 BC, Egypt became a Roman province.

During the 4th century, the Church of Alexandria (*El Iskandariya*) was established in Egypt. The descendants of its founders are known today as the Copts. In 639 AD, Arab invaders brought Islam to Egypt; more than a religion, it became a way of life. Cairo was established as *El Qahirah* in 969 AD; it soon became the capital of the Muslim Fatimid Empire, which established lucrative trade links. In 970 AD, the El Azhar Mosque was built, evolving into a university, and it has remained a prominent institution that preserves Islamic theology and philosophy.

In 1192, Salah el Din dethroned the Fatimids and took control. The Mamelukes – originally slaves – ruled Egypt until the Ottomans arrived.

Between 1517 and 1914, Egypt was an Ottoman province, but decentralisation allowed Mameluke princes – *beys* – to retain power. During that time, Egypt's best artisans and craftsmen were taken to the imperial capital, Istanbul, then known as Constantinople. Ottoman rule was temporarily interrupted when Napoleon occupied Egypt from 1798 to 1801. The British then helped the Ottomans drive the French out of Egypt.

In 1805, Mohammed Ali – an Albanian mercenary in the Ottoman army – was appointed governor of Egypt; he leased the country's semi-independence from the Ottomans. Under this arrangement, Egyptian leaders, known as *khedives*, paid a tax to the sultan in exchange for political power. Legally, the *khedives* were viceroys, ruling on behalf of the Ottoman sultan, but in practice they were very autonomous.

Entrepreneur & His Cotton

Mohammed Ali was greatly influenced by the industrialisation of Europe and he was keen to develop industry in Egypt. He pushed for the establishment of cotton mills, oil mills, paper mills, rice mills, silk mills, wool mills, sugar refineries, iron foundries, tanneries, printing works and shipyards. Much later, industrialisation was accelerated by Talaat Harb, the founder of *Banque Misr*.

In 1836, steamships began to link Egypt with Bombay. In 1853, Egypt became the fifth country in the world, and the first one east of Europe, to establish a railway infrastructure. The following year, French diplomat Ferdinand de Lesseps proposed the construction of the Suez Canal, a 102 mile-long waterway across the Isthmus of Suez, linking the Mediterranean Sea to the Red Sea. Since its opening in 1869, the Suez Canal greatly facilitated trade between Europe and the Far East.

© 2000 by Leo Paul Dana

The Suez Canal

French became the language of business and of high society in Egypt, and English influence followed. The ruler, Khedive Ismail – descendent of Mohammed Ali – encountered financial difficulties and in 1875 the British government bought the controlling shares of the Suez Canal. In 1888, the Convention of Constantinople made Britain the guarantor of a neutral Suez Canal.

Until 1906, the border between Egypt and the Ottoman Empire was a straight line from Suez to Rafah, thereby giving Egypt the Mediterranean coastline of the Sinai Desert, but not the southern Sinai. A Turco-British agreement, in 1906, placed the remainder of the Sinai Desert under Anglo-Egyptian administration. However, it was agreed that the Sinai would remain legally part of the Ottoman Empire.

In 1913, Britain declared Egypt a British Protectorate and deposed the *khedive*, Abbas Hilmi, who was accused of being pro-Ottoman. Abbas Hilmi's uncle, Hussein Kamil, replaced him. When Hussein Kamil died, he was succeeded by his brother Ahmed Fouad, later known as Sultan Ahmed Fouad Pasha.

© 2000 by Leo Paul Dana

Peasants at Work

Egypt was declared an independent country on February 28, 1922, and on March 16, Fouad was crowned King of Egypt. In 1923, Turkey renounced its right to Egypt, according to the Treaty of Lausanne; Article 17 stipulated that the treaty was based on the international boundaries as they were on November 5, 1914. Thus, the Turks technically relinquished Egypt, excluding the Sinai.

In April 1936, King Fouad was succeeded by his son, Farouk. While the elite prospered, life for the peasants was hard. Up until WWII, Egypt had the highest death rate in the world, and four out of five Egyptians had bilharzia, malaria or both.

Above: The National Bank of Egypt Was a British Institution

Below: Postage Stamp Showing Farouk and a DC-3 Over Egypt

King Farouk was forced to abdicate in July 1952. He was the last descendent of Mohammed Ali to rule Egypt.

Postage Stamp with the King's Face Barred After His Abdication

In 1952, a series of land reforms abolished the quasi-feudal system that had survived since Ottoman rule. These decrees reduced private agricultural land holdings to 80 acres and subsequently to 20 hectares. This enabled the government to redistribute farmland to peasant farmers (see also Nasser, 1954). Although the Copyright Law (Law N°354) was passed in 1954, Egypt refused to consider itself bound by Article 33 of the Berne Convention.

In 1956, Colonel Gamal Abdel Nasser became president. His dream was to industrialise Egypt and for this he needed energy. A hydroelectric dam at Aswan could greatly increase power potential, but would cost a fortune to build. Nasser felt he could best accumulate capital by confiscating the revenues of the Suez Canal Company. He therefore nationalised the Suez Canal, which was majority-owned by the British government. This led to an armed conflict. Despite military defeat, Egypt was saved by intervention from the United States and the Soviet Union.

Nasser proceeded with the Aswan Dam, a project which drowned the entire region called Egyptian Nubia. Its inhabitants, the Nubians, are an ethnic minority of mixed Arab and Negro blood. Paying the price of progress, these people were forced to leave their villages, with only necessities, leaving animals and belongings behind.

As of 1956, private enterprise suffered a serious drawback in Egypt. Many Jewish and Christian entrepreneurs fled the country, and assets were confiscated. In 1958, the United Arab Republic – a union between Egypt and Syria – was established. Between 1959 and 1961, Egypt's economy was radically socialised. In 1961, banking, foreign trade and insurance became nationalised sectors. All private shipping agencies were nationalised that year. Most manufacturers and wholesalers were also nationalised, while heavy regulation restrained private enterprises. Furthermore, Law N°15 of 1963 banned the ownership of agricultural land by foreigners.

The Ades Building in Cairo, Built by Jewish Entrepreneurs

The nation's anti-Western stance led to a decrease in tourism during the 1960s. The 6-Day War in 1967 also hurt the economy.

© 2000 by Leo Paul Dana

War Closed the Suez Canal

Mostert (1972) predicted a revolution in Egypt. In October 1973, Egypt attacked Israel, launching another expensive war. This came to be known as the Yom Kippur War.

Policy Reforms

Peace with Israel – discussed in Chapter 8 – ushered in a new era of development, and during the 1990s, Egypt embarked on a comprehensive economic reform programme, involving fiscal and monetary tightening, exchange rate liberalisation and price deregulation. This led to macroeconomic stability, promoting foreign direct investment and fostering economic growth. In 1995, an Israeli-Egyptian joint venture began construction on Egypt's first privately-owned oil refinery.

Peaceful Border Between Egypt and Israel

Legislative reforms, in 1996, enhanced the environment for business, accelerating regulatory reform, privatisation, and the liberalisation of trade. Law N°11 abolished the stamp tax on company incorporation. Law N°227 abolished inheritance taxes. Law N°231 eliminated the need for Egyptians to obtain permits to work for foreign organisations. Also in 1996, the capital gains tax on securities was withdrawn.

© 2000 by Leo Paul Dana

The Government Facilitated Business

In 1997, Presidential Decree N°284 organised the General Authority for Investment & Free Trade Zones. Firms in Free Trade Zones enjoy duty-free status on imports and unlimited tax exemption on profits.

Law N°8 of 1997 introduced further business incentives to attract investment to Egypt. This legislation reduced bureaucratic paperwork hurdles, and introduced corporate tax holidays. With the new law, a company can be incorporated in 24 hours and output is not subject to price controls. The same legislation offered new ventures tax holidays of up to twenty years, along with tariff reductions on imported equipment and machinery. In addition, firms were exempted from existing labour laws.

Welcoming Western Investment

The year 1998 saw the creation of 2,187 new companies, a seven-fold increase compared to 1995 start-ups. Also in 1998, Law N°1 liberalised shipping, while Law N°162 reduced taxes on international airline tickets. That same year the National Democratic Party recommended "to maximise the role SMEs can play in boosting the competitiveness of the national economy, especially in providing real job opportunities."

© 2000 by Leo Paul Dana

Cairo International Airport

The Small Business Sector

Small and micro-enterprises – defined as those with up to 14 workers – make up 98.7% of non-agricultural private firms in Egypt, and account for 66% of the nation's employment. The small business sector is considered to be the nation's most efficient means to create jobs, as it is labour-intensive and requires limited investment and infrastructure. In Egypt, small enterprises realise more value-adding per investment dollar than do larger firms with the same.

Several organisations encourage and assist small business in Egypt. The Government of Egypt Social Fund for Development was established in 1991, to mitigate the adverse social effects of the Economic Reform & Structural Adjustment Programme. The fund was originally established as a social safety net, but its mission was soon enlarged, making it the vanguard of economic empowerment. The Social Fund for Development introduced the Enterprise Development Programme to assist women, young graduates and artisans, to launch new enterprises. The programme also provided working capital to existing entrepreneurs. Sample projects are listed in Table 6.1.

PROJECT TITLE	OBJECTIVE	OPPORTUNITIES
Handicraft Expansion	To support existing handicrafts and to assist in establishing new handicraft enterprises, creating jobs for youth	70,000 jobs
Credit Guarantee	To stimulate growth of small enterprises	6,000 jobs
Small Enterprise Development	To grant loans to young entrepreneurs in agro-sector	5,000 jobs
Sayeda Zainab	To assist artisans in Sayeda Zainab	350 jobs

Table 6.1 Sample Projects of the Enterprise Development Programme

The Enterprise Development Programme evolved into the Small-Enterprise Development Organisation, a financially sustainable entity, with a mandate of enlarging the small-business sector by 100,000 jobs per year. The Industrial Development Bank of Egypt, the National Bank for Development and the National Bank of Egypt also support the expansion of small firms in Egypt.

Many entrepreneurs in Egypt operate in the informal economy. The informal sector provides several important social functions. It allows the creation of jobs with limited capital; it provides employment for every level of skill; it enables apprentices to learn on the job; it permits development with limited technology; and it diffuses income. This sector produces 30% of Egypt's GNP.

Small-scale Operators Fulfil an Important Role in Distribution

Credit for Entrepreneurs

Egyptian banks have traditionally shared a negative perception of small business; entrepreneurs requesting loans are asked for considerable collateral and guarantees, and until recently, few small firms succeeded in obtaining formal capital. Yet, the informal sector in Egypt employs more direct labour per unit of capital than do larger firms of the formal sector. As well, informal enterprises in Egypt make due with unskilled, and at best semi-skilled, labour under the guidance of a skilled entrepreneur. Small firms in Egypt have a comparative advantage with their high labour-to-capital ratio. This is what led to the creation of credit programmes to assist informal entrepreneurs in the bazaar economy – individuals who have no collateral, no traditional security, no salary and no experience with banks. Many of these individuals do not even have a license, registration or a workshop permit.

Artisans in an Informal Workshop

The National Bank for Development introduced the Rural Small Enterprise Programme, and the Small Enterprise Credit Programme (SECP). The SECP provides loans to artisans and to other participants in the informal sector, on the basis of their ability to service the loan. Loans vary in amount from £E250 (Egyptian pounds) – under $100 – to £E100,000. Borrowers are selected based on their cash flow. Artisans, itinerant traders and home-based industries are amongst the 155 different informal activities financed by the SECP. According to interviews, conducted by the author at the National Bank for Development, there have been almost no defaults.

A study by Dana (2000) found that 90% of the borrowers are male. This is not surprising, as Egyptian culture does not support entrepreneurship among women. Nonetheless, counter to cultural values, funds are available specifically for female entrepreneurs in Egypt.

The Canadian International Development Agency (CIDA) and UNICEF have formed partnerships with the National Bank for Development to manage special credit programmes geared to women living in Upper Egypt, in Luxor and in Qena in particular.

Among the other sources of assistance to entrepreneurs in Egypt is the Alexandria Businessmen's Association, which provides loans without collateral, in addition to technical support and training in costing, pricing, accounting and production planning. The borrowers – whose performance is monitored – are charged commercial lending rates.

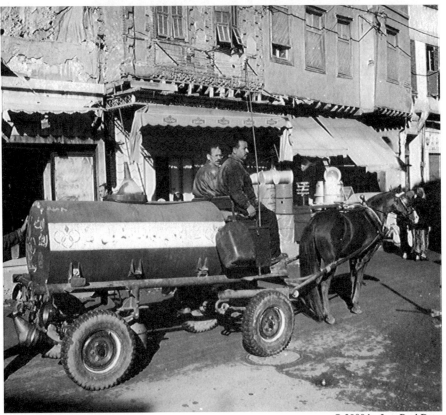

© 2000 by Leo Paul Dana

Small-scale in Alexandria

As well, the Credit Guarantee Corporation is involved in raising the productivity of small-scale enterprises, and in helping them improve their credit ratings. USAID is also involved in small business promotion in Egypt. It introduced the Commodity Import Programme & Sciences & Technology Project. The United States Investment Promotion Office provides expertise to entrepreneurs. In addition, the Freidrich Ebert Stiftung – a German-funded foundation – assists craftsmen in the furniture, leather and metalwork sectors.

© 2000 by Leo Paul Dana

Repairing Shoes Along a Sidewalk

The Bedouins

The Bedouins are a distinct ethnic group in Egypt, and these people tend not to marry outside their community. There is much pressure for a girl to marry within her family; a first cousin is a perfect candidate. Among these people, clitoridectomy was widely practised until the 1960s and polygamy is still common.

© 2000 by Leo Paul Dana

Bedouin of the Sinai

There are important differences among Bedouin groups. The members of most tribes have traditionally been self-employed, and they have looked down at the Jebaliya tribe. The Jebaliyas are mountain people of the southern Sinai Desert and other Bedouins have considered them inferior due to alleged Christian ancestry. Furthermore, they have been criticised by other tribes, for earning wage labour at the Santa Katerina Monastery, rather than relying on traditional self-employment. More recently, Jebaliyas have acquired land in wadis, and their economy now includes income from orchards as well as livestock. Nevertheless, they still require permission from Christian monks, in order to establish a business in the vicinity of the Santa Katerina Monastery.

There continues to be a marked division of labour among the Bedouins. While men have duties external to the home, women are expected to do all of the household chores, taking care of domestic needs, caring for the children, milling wheat, baking bread, churning milk into butter, and making cheese. Women are also expected to weave carpets, to embroider clothes, and to gather brush for fire-making. In addition, they tend to domestic animals and graze the flocks.

For the Bedouins of coastal areas, pearl-diving has brought considerable income. Fishing is important for subsistence, and for sale. There are special rituals for the angel of the sea.

Toward the Future

By the end of the 20th century, Egypt had lowered tariffs, eliminated most subsidies, introduced market-pricing principles and abolished trade quotas. The private sector accounted for two-thirds of economic activity in Egypt. The introduction of business-friendly legislation, macro-economic stability and the acceleration of non-oil exports suggest that Egypt will enjoy high growth rates in the years to come. Income tax on dividends has been abolished and all export quotas have been eliminated. The service sector is growing rapidly, the stock market has been reflecting success and entrepreneurs have shown themselves to be innovative agents of progress. Even crop productivity is improving. Wheat production has increased from 1.47 tons per feddan[3] during the late 20th century, to 2.35 tons per feddan today.

---

[3] A feddan is equal to 1.037 acres.

Making Jam for Export

Profitability, in Egypt, is enhanced by the abundance of low-cost labour. A typical unskilled worker earns $100 per month. An average hourly wage in Egypt converts to $1.30, compared to the equivalent of $14.20 in the United Kingdom, $16.10 in Italy, $16.90 in France and $26.50 in Germany.

In order to match the growth of the workforce in Egypt, there is a need to create 450,000 jobs annually; this would be possible with an 11% growth in exports. To facilitate this, Egypt joined the Southern and East African trade bloc, COMESA. As well, Egypt signed an agreement with Turkey, to increase trade between the two countries.

Physically closer is Israel, which is already Egypt's second biggest trading partner in the Middle East and North Africa. Each year, Egypt sells 2 million tons of crude oil to Israel, while non-oil trade has been approaching $100 million. Studies suggest that half a million Israeli tourists could visit Egypt each year, adding another $750 million to the economy.

Fibre optic technology has improved international communication links, and Telecom Egypt has plans to increase phone lines by one million a year. Meanwhile, the state plans to convert 1.4 million hectares of desert to farmland, by 2017.

© 2000 by Leo Paul Dana

Port Said, Gateway to Africa, Asia, and the Mediterranean Sea

Chapter 7

The Hellenic Republic

The Greeks were calling to each other on the walls of
Troy, as the ducks cry out at dusk on the plains of Asia.
— Homer's Iliad

Introduction

Greece, locally known as *Hellas*, is situated on the southern part of the Balkan Peninsula, with islands stretching into the Aegean and the Ionian. The country holds a strategic position among the Balkans. Covering an area of 131,957 square kilometres, the nation shares borders with Albania, Bulgaria, the Former Yugoslav Republic of Macedonia (FYROM) and Turkey. While Albania is the subject of Chapter 4 and Turkey of Chapter 13, Bulgaria is treated separately in Dana (1999a) and FYROM in Dana (1998).

Emigration from Greece, during the 20th century, led numerous Greek entrepreneurs to become successful entrepreneurs in Australia, Canada, New Zealand, the United States and beyond. In time, family links evolved into important networks for international business. While technology is exported from Greece to its neighbours, Greeks tend to prefer more lucrative trade with distant, but wealthier, business partners. The Greek merchant marine — the largest fleet in the world — constitutes about a quarter of the European Union shipping capacity.

Greece, today, has booming financial and technology sectors. While much of the Greek economy is modern and international in nature, the government also recognises the importance of preserving the skills of traditional artisans. The handicraft and artisan sector is given special attention in Greece, and this has helped the economic development of rural areas, while avoiding uncontrolled industrialisation and urbanisation.

103

© 2000 by Leo Paul Dana

Athens, Canada: Greek Entrepreneurs Settled in Canada

Historical Overview

In the Aegean Sea, south of the Greek mainland, lie several islands with rich traditions of trade. The Minoans had an advanced European civilisation in Crete, about 4,500 years ago. These people exported wine and olives around the Mediterranean; they bought gold from Egypt and tin from Spain, and became very skilled metalworkers. Not far away, in the group of islands known as the Cyclades, the Cycladic civilisation developed, between 3000 BC and 1000 BC.

When Phoenician merchants brought papyrus from Byblos (north of Beirut) to Greece, Greek artisans began producing books. Their word for book – *biblio* – is derived from the name of Byblos, the Levantine town. Later, the English "Bible" was derived from the same.

In 166 BC, under Roman rule, the Greek island of Delos became a free port. The island subsequently became a hub for cargoes travelling between Europe, Africa and Asia. It had a sprawling bazaar where slaves were bought and sold, as were glass, ivory, papyrus, parchment, perfumes and textiles.

Until the 15th century, the Duchy of Naxos, was an important local power. Then came Ottoman rule.

In 1770, Greece sided with Russia against the Ottoman Empire. In the 1821, the Greeks launched their War of Independence, and on March 10, 1829, the Protocol of London created modern Greece.

When it was decided that Greece would become a monarchy, a king was brought in from Bavaria. He was forced to step down, in 1862, in favour of George I of Denmark. The borders of Greece were expanded during the Balkan Wars of 1912-1913.

After World War II, civil war erupted in Greece. The country found itself poor and unstable. This contributed to an exodus of Greeks, to North America and Australia in particular. Nevertheless, a strong work ethic helped rebuild Greece.

The military came into power in 1967, and the monarchy was abolished in 1974. A new constitution gave Greece a presidential parliamentary system, in 1975. Access to European Union accelerated economic development in Greece.

The Economy

The English word "economy" comes from the Greek *oikonomos*, literally meaning "law of the house." As was the case in much of Europe, the traditional economic unit in Greece was the family farm. In coastal areas, and in the islands, fishing activities supplemented agriculture and stock-raising, the primary sources of income until the late 1950s. Sheep were important for their wool and for their meat, while goats were prized for their milk from which feta cheese was made. Not only valleys, but also hills were farmed. The cultivation of mountain slopes was made possible by the establishment of terrace farms, separated from one another by low stone walls, known as *pezoules*. In less fertile areas, bee-keeping resulted in the thriving production of thyme honey.

© 2000 by Leo Paul Dana

Goats Were Prized for Their Milk

The Greek Orthodox Church encouraged strong ties within the extended family, and within the community. This strengthened the family farm and enhanced the development of numerous family enterprises. Priests – forming a part of the extended family, and playing an important role in the community – often became involved in business.

Greek enterprises traditionally conducted relatively little business with firms in neighbouring countries – namely Albania, Bulgaria, Turkey and the Yugoslav republics. Instead, the Greeks concentrated on trading with wealthier trading partners, including western Europeans, and North Americans. About 25% of the nation's trade takes place with Germans, and 10% with Italians. Also significant is the trade done between entrepreneurs in Greece and Greeks residing overseas.

© 2000 by Leo Paul Dana

Rhodes Has Italian Connections

In recent years, Greek banks and construction firms have been at the forefront of economic development in the Balkans. Yet, parts of Greece have succeeded in retaining their romantic charm. While the infrastructure has been significantly improved since the nation's entry into the European Economic Community, caravans of mules are still used to transport merchandise in distant mountain villages.

Where the Mule is Efficient

On some Aegean islands, a sheer rock wall separates the harbour from the village(s). Ascension can be made by foot, but mules are the most practical means of transporting bulky and/or heavy goods. In this setting, the location of a business establishment not strategically planned in the Western sense. Personal relationships dominate business. Since competition is limited, villagers displace themselves, to wherever the supply is being sold. In some villages, cheese is sold in a shop; elsewhere, the only place to buy cheese is at somebody's house. The church is central to the village and many priests are involved in business. Partnerships often involve relatives, as the extended family is very important in Greek society. As is the case in many trades, fishing is an occupation that is often passed on from father to son.

Until recently, innovative technology has played a relatively minor role in competitiveness. Rather than concentrating on pushing its entrepreneurs away from traditional activities and toward more sophisticated technologies, a priority in Greece has been, and continues to be, the encouragement of artisans to maintain their handicraft activities.

Respecting Tradition

The Development Centre of Arts and Crafts, known as KEBA, and the National Organisation of Greek Handicrafts (EOEX), were both pioneers in promoting the handicraft activities of artisans in Greece. Today, the principal body doing this is the Hellenic Organisation for Medium and Small-Size Enterprises and Handicrafts (EOMMEX).

EOMMEX

Dana (1999b) discusses EOMMEX and its activities. The non-profit organisation was established in 1977, by Law N°707, under the supervision of the Ministry of Industry, Research, Technology and Trade. This legislation was subsequently amended in 1984 and in 1991.

Funded by the European Union as well as by the national government, EOMMEX is responsible for maintaining a favourable environment for entrepreneurship development. The organisation lobbies to enhance the economic climate for small enterprises. Also, EOMMEX trains entrepreneurs and provides them with financial assistance and marketing services.

EOMMEX focuses special efforts to encourage the artisanal handicraft and arts-and-crafts sectors. It provides artistic and technical assistance, in addition to marketing services. Specific projects focus on ceramics, costume jewellery, knitting, lace, sculpturing and the even the building of sea vessels.

Greeks Have Long Been Talented Ship-builders

The EOMMEX Training Department organises seminars and field visits, during which artistic and technical advice is provided. The Technical Assistance Department is available for consultation with respect to location selection and infrastructure support; it also assists with applications for grants. The Marketing Department conducts market research and trains artisans in the commercialisation of handicrafts. Artisans are encouraged to participate in commercial fairs. Offices in Frankfurt and in New York help with the international marketing of crafts. Furthermore, an EOMMEX matchmaking service links Greek artisans with import houses overseas.

Also, there is a special programme for handicraft development in rural areas. Thus, EOMMEX has been contributing to a healthy handicraft sector, throughout Greece. The organisation's activities have been enhancing job satisfaction, as well as profitability, in rural areas. This makes it possible to curb urbanisation, while preserving culture and assuring a bright economic future.

Tourism & Change

Barth (1963; 1967) explains how entrepreneurs can become agents of social change. In Greece, tourism led entrepreneurs to transform the economy of some regions. Dana (1999d) analyses the case of Ios, among the southernmost of the Cyclades, situated 107 nautical miles from the port of Piraeus. Locally known as *Nios*, this island, with 82 kilometres of shoreline, covers an area of 108 square kilometres.

Archaeological findings reveal that a community flourished here, since the early Cycladic period. The Phoenicians later called the island Phoenicia. After the Phoenicians, Ios was home to Ionians, Romans, Byzantines, Franks, Venetians and Ottomans. The name Ios was probably derived from the word *ion*, Greek for violets, which are prevalent here, each spring.

Fertile valleys on this island include Aghia Theodoti, Kambos, Manganari, Mylopotas, and Psathi. The Panokampo Valley is noted for its olive trees and for its grapevines. Highly productive olive trees gave rise to five oil presses on this Cycladic island. Grapevines are valuable not only for their grapes but also for their leaves, which are used in traditional Greek cooking.

Ios, One the Cyclades

Abundant harvests of cotton, in Ios, facilitated the development of a profitable textile factory. The firm produced fabrics from the cotton of local plantations.

Farmers, artisans and tradesmen prospered on Ios. Tools used in agriculture were generally made on the island, by the self-employed ironmonger. Several windmills were built on Ios, to grind wheat. A baker made fresh bread and he paid his staff in kind, rather than in cash. The wealthiest entrepreneurs of Ios were perhaps the barrel-makers who crafted barrels for wine. Wishing a boy to become a barrel-maker was synonymous with wishing him prosperity from entrepreneurship.

Ios is also rich in emery and in marble. Up until World War II, small-scale mines, with up to eighty people in all, extracted emery, pyrite and sulphur on this island.

Ios Windmills

During the 1960s, the first tourists came to Ios. This launched a new industry on the island. Miles of pristine beaches, surrounded by turquoise waters, made Ios a favourite tourist destination. According to the Ios Port Authority, almost 15,000 holidaymakers visit each summer.

For the islanders, this caused dramatic changes. The arrival of outsiders introduced new opportunities. Entrepreneurs in Ios soon realised that foreigners were accustomed to paying higher prices in their own countries, than those being charged on the island. Although merchants had traditionally used a cost-plus method of pricing, it became more interesting to charge the highest prices that the market could bear – and tourists were willing to pay inflated prices.

During the initial stages of economic change, only a few entrepreneurs internalised the cognitive and normative themes intrinsic to the evolving environment. A variety of causal variables may explain why these individuals were open to change. Some people, with entrepreneurial personalities, may have resented conforming to established norms. Others may have been maladjusted to the traditional status quo. By internalising new economic structures, they prospered.

Eventually, traditional enterprise, in Ios, faded, as more and more islanders shifted their occupations to service the tourist trade. During the 1960s, the factory making spectacles closed down. So did the textile factory and this caused a drop in demand for local cotton. Farmers abandoned their plantations, in favour of more profitable occupations. Hotels and restaurants took the place of terrace farms and grapevines. The ironmongers and barrel-makers disappeared. The oil presses stopped operating, as did the mills. Gone too are the kiln workers who used to produce lime for whitewashing traditional houses. Only one shoemaker remains.

Meanwhile, tourism has flourished. Beer, pizza and hot dogs are being sold where local wine and *kadaifi* were once the norm. In the not-so-distant past, fresh lamb was the staple meat; now processed ham is brought in, packaged. On this island upon which figs, oranges and pears grew in abundance, most of the jams and juices are now imported.

Feta cheese was first developed in Greece, and by definition is made from goat's milk; for the tourists, a cheese made from cow's milk and called "feta," was brought here from Denmark. Only in 1997, the European Commission deemed that feta must be Greek in order to be feta.

Not all change is for the better. Meltemi Co. announces "radical watersports action." Indeed, wake-boarding, water skiing, and tube rides are but a few of the activities that share the once-crystal-clear water. Hydrofoils have also arrived. Psathi Beach, on Ios, is among the most important breeding ground for the Mediterranean sea-turtle. Not surprisingly, countless turtles and fish get injured. Islanders who once fished in these waters now eat canned fish from overseas. Baseball caps and wet-suits have replaced Greek fisherman hats.

Just a few years ago, Greek girls shyly watched Canadians, Germans, Swedes and members of other ethnic groups, getting drunk, flirting and sunbathing in the nude. Today, the boundaries of ethnicity have faded.

When the sea is dirty, many escape to overcrowded swimming pools at beachside hotels and campgrounds. One should be careful when walking, as numerous broken beer bottles are scattered on the roads, steps and beaches.

As tourism development has turned the inhabitants, of this island, away from agriculture, from fishing and from other traditional activities, fertile fields are being taken over by weeds. Tourism has become the principal source of income.

© 2000 by Leo Paul Dana

Road to the Top

Toward the Future

Greece has evolved from a poor country 50 years ago, to a modern economy set for the future. Furthermore, assistance from the European Union is greatly accelerating the economic development of Greece. On March 9, 2000, Greece formally applied for membership in the European Monetary Union. As the telecom monopoly of OTE expires, on-line commerce may grow exponentially.

© 2000 by Leo Paul Dana

The Port of Piraeus

While gaining from the experience of others, Greece is being careful not to repeat errors already made elsewhere. While other countries have been suffering the effects of rapid urbanisation, Greece has recognised the advantage of keeping rural people in the countryside. To this end, the state assists rural artisans, thereby contributing to regional development and social stability.

The Dawn of a New Era

Chapter 8

The State of Israel

*Silicon Valley really has only one rival outside the United States –
Israel. Wall Street knows it.* — *Newsweek*

Introduction

Israel covers 20,325 square kilometres. Its neighbours are Egypt, Jordan, Lebanon, Syria and the Palestinian Authority territories. While Hebrew and Arabic are official languages in Israel, English, Russian, French and Spanish are widely spoken.

During most of its history since independence, Israel was governed by its Labour Party, with socialist policies. The economy was dominated by agriculture and by labour-intensive industries. More recently, the state focused on educating its youth and in integrating highly-skilled immigrants. As a result, Israel ranks third in the industrialised world (behind the United States and the Netherlands), in terms of university degrees per capita. Israel has 135 scientists and technicians per 10,000 workers – more than has any other industrialised country. Coupled with high expenditures on research and development (R & D), this has transformed Israel into a highly advanced society, with a technology-driven economy, a mere 2% of which is derived from agriculture. Israel became the first, and only, country in the world to have free trade agreements with the European Union, and with the three NAFTA members. The state has diplomatic relations with 160 nations.

Prudent fiscal and monetary policies, the liberalisation of trade, deregulation, privatisation, and the removal of exchange controls, coupled with the peace process, have greatly boosted the economy. Israel, today, is characterised by an excellent infrastructure, per capita GDP at par with western European economies, and growth rates as high as Asia's tigers.

Israel was the first nation to launch m-commerce. This new technology makes it possible to use mobile phones to activate fuel dispensers and to pay for petrol at service stations.

Historical Overview

> The Land of Israel was the birthplace of the Jewish people. Here their spiritual, religious and national identity was shaped. Here they achieved independence and created a culture of national and universal significance. Here they wrote and gave the Bible to the world...
>
> – Declaration of the Establishment of the State of Israel published in the *Official Gazette,* May 14, 1948

In Biblical times, Israel stretched from Egypt to the Euphrates River. The Bible tells us that Moses led the people of Israel out of slavery in Egypt, and under the leadership of Joshua, the children of Israel were led to the promised land of milk and honey which the sons of Jacob had left a few generations earlier. The Jewish kingdoms of Judaea and Israel were founded in Eretz Yisrael – the Land of Israel – and the tribe of Zebulun specialised in commerce. Foreign trade accelerated economic development, especially under King Solomon.

In 586 BC, Judaea was overrun by Babylon and for forty-seven years many of the people were in exile, until King Cyrus of Persia allowed them to return and restore Jewish statehood, that in which Jesus lived. This second commonwealth was destroyed by the Romans in the year 70 AD, at which time Jerusalem came to be known as *Aelia Capitolina* and the Jewish kingdom of Judaea was renamed *Syria Palaestina*.

Later, the Byzantine Empire ruled over the Holy Land. Then came the Muslim expansion, under which the Islamic state of the Rashidun khalifes covered the entire area. The Crusaders invaded in 1089, and subsequently established Christian sovereignty over the Holy Land. In Jerusalem, they exterminated the Muslim communities, they converted the Dome of the Rock into a church, and they transformed the Al-Asqa Mosque into a royal residence.

©2000 by Leo Paul Dana

Jerusalem - ירושלים

The Crusaders were followed by the Egyptian Mamelukes, who ruled the region from 1291 until the arrival of the Ottomans. Under Ottoman governance, which lasted from 1516 to 1917, Israel was known as Palestine – a province of the Ottoman Empire.

The Bedouins – tribal groups whose traditional lifestyle was nomadic pastoralism – bred camels, goats and sheep, for a livelihood. The sheikhs – powerful leaders at the time – also charged caravans for passage across the desert. There were two principal communities of Bedouins in Ottoman Palestine. Those in the north were of Syrian ancestry. Those in the south – in the Negev Desert – had their origins in tribes that came from the Sinai Desert and the Arabian Peninsula. The two groups were not related; they spoke dissimilar dialects. Those in the Negev Desert usually did not register their lands; this exempted them from real estate tax. By the 1850s, the traditional pastoral economy of the Bedouins began evolving toward a mixed agricultural and pastoral economy. As the Ottomans began building the railroad to Egypt, many Bedouins were attracted to wage labour. In time, the old elite – illiterate, but powerful sheikhs – gave way to a new order.

©2000 by Leo Paul Dana

Bedouins of the Negev Desert

Between 1876 and 1908, Sultan Abdul Hamid II encouraged the migration of loyal subjects, to outlying areas of the Ottoman Empire. A new policy, adopted in 1878, exempted migrants from taxes for twelve years. Muslims from North Africa and Circassians from the Caucasus Mountains subsequently relocated to the Galilee. Also, Muslim Bosnians migrated to Caesaria.

Meanwhile in Europe:

> A whole series of special taxes were invented and enforced against Jews...meat cost a third more to the Jews...a percentage tax was levied upon all rents received by Jews and on profits...printing presses owned by Jews paid annually...the Jewish head of a family had to pay a special tax...Jewish youths were stripped of practically all safeguards and legal reservations... (Harold, 1892, pp. 28-29).

©2000 by Leo Paul Dana

Hebrew Community Centre in Moldavia

An Austro-Hungarian journalist, Theodore Herzl, observed the inequality of Jews while covering the trial of Alfred Dreyfus – a Jewish officer wrongly accused of betraying the French army. Herzl's response was that the Jews should purchase land in order to establish their own country. His book, *The Jewish State*, was published in 1896, suggesting the mass immigration of Jews to their own homeland.

Political Zionists then aimed to seek political recognition and legitimacy, to be followed by mass immigration. In 1897, Herzl organised the First Zionist Congress, in Basle, Switzerland. Thus was born the World Zionist Organisation, which in 1901 created the Jewish National Fund to raise funds for the purchase of real estate in Ottoman Palestine. Financial assistance came from Jewish philanthropists, including Sir Moses Montefiore and Baron Edmond de Rothschild.

Commanded by General Sir Edmund Allenby, the British captured Ottoman Palestine during World War I. They took Beersheva on October 31, 1917, and on November 2 the British Foreign Secretary – Arthur James Balfour – signed the document which came to be known as the Balfour Declaration (see Exhibit 8.1). With this declaration, England committed itself to facilitate the establishment of a Jewish homeland. The British proceeded to take Gaza, on November 7, and Jaffa on November 16. Finally, the British occupied Jerusalem, on December 11, 1917.

The Treaty of Versailles set up a system of mandates, for the administration of former possessions of Germany and of the Ottoman Empire. On April 25, 1920, the San Remo Conference confirmed the pledge contained in the Balfour Declaration, concerning the establishment of a Jewish national home in Palestine. It was at this conference that the mandate for Palestine – including the Golan Heights – was given to Britain; the basis for the British regime, in Palestine, was the Balfour Declaration. The mandate was ratified by the Council of the League of Nations, on June 24, 1922. France backed the idea of a Jewish homeland in Palestine, and the United States soon followed suit. Herzl's (1896) book was soon widely read in French (1926). In 1923, Britain ceded the Golan to the French mandate, discussed in Chapters 10 & 12.

Although the League of Nations had recognised the legality of the Balfour Declaration, the British were not pressed to conform to it. The land in question was divided. The eastern part – covering over 80% of the area of British Palestine – was severed from the area to which the provision of the Balfour Declaration would apply. Eastern Palestine was renamed Trans-Jordan, and later Jordan, the subject of Chapter 9.

© 2000 by Leo Paul Dana

Montefiore's Windmill in Jerusalem

Between the two world wars, many Jews came to what remained of British Palestine, in order to escape anti-Semitism in Europe. Not all were welcome, however, and in 1929, raids nearly wiped out the flourishing Jewish community of Hebron (on the West Bank of the Jordan River). In 1932, 1934 and 1936, the Levant Fair was held in Tel Aviv. Its purpose was to promote trade.

Foreign Office,
November 2nd, 1917.

Dear Lord Rothschild,

        I have much pleasure in conveying to you, on behalf of His Majesty's Government, the following declaration of sympathy with Jewish Zionist aspirations which has been submitted to, and approved by the cabinet.

    'His Majesty's Government view with favour the establishment in Palestine of a national home for the Jewish people, and will use their best endeavours to facilitate the achievement of this object, it being clearly understood that nothing shall be done which may prejudice the civil and religious rights of existing non-Jewish communities in Palestine, or the rights and political status enjoyed by Jews in any other country'.

        I should be grateful if you would bring this declaration to the knowledge of the Zionist Federation.

Exhibit 8.1. The Balfour Declaration
(Original in the British Museum, London)

    As persecution in Europe worsened, more Jews came to British Palestine. Large-scale immigration, however, prompted a series of Arab terrorist acts, beginning in 1936.

    The British kept a tight hold on the economy. They went as far as disallowing Bedouin Arabs from collecting salt from Sodom. Meanwhile, the camel trade dwindled with the arrival of the automobile. Formerly wealthy people became impoverished. Many went to work in Jewish agricultural settlements, for wages.

In 1939, Great Britain was strategically concerned about retaining, and even strengthening, its friendship with the Arabs. The population of Arab lands was one hundred million, and it would be a valuable asset to England to have them as allies on the eve of a war. The MacDonald White Paper of 1939 confirmed Britain's pro-Arab policy, by restricting Jewish immigration and land purchase.

In 1947, United Nations Resolution 181 proposed a partition of British Palestine, which would result in an Arab Palestine and a Jewish homeland. Nine percent of the area of Ottoman Palestine was allotted to the Jews, while the rest would yield the Arabs two Arab states, *i.e.*, Jordan and Palestine.

A Country Reborn

On May 14, 1948, Israel's declaration of independence was met by a military invasion, which became known as the Independence War. Azzam Pasha, Secretary General of the Arab League, exclaimed: "This will be a war of extermination and momentous massacre." While Egypt took control of the Gaza Strip and Jordan succeeded in occupying East Jerusalem and the West Bank (of the Jordan River), no Palestine was born. Thus, British Palestine was carved up, but not according to Resolution 181.

Jews from Arab lands soon arrived in Israel, escaping religious persecution in their respective countries of origin. Among the newcomers, many identified themselves as Arabic-speaking Jews rather than as Israelis. Perceiving a lack of social mobility in mainstream Israeli society, many of these immigrants set up new ventures in Israel.

At the time, the state regulated many sectors, and taxes were high, as military expenditures needed to be financed. The socialist policies of the Labour-led government were not conducive to entrepreneurship.

Meanwhile, a communal form of enterprise flourished. Known as the *kibbutz*, this institution involves a communal sharing of work (as per one's ability), profit (as per one's needs), child-rearing and leisure time, on communal grounds. Meals and child-care are provided. It used to be that the *kibbutz* economy was based on agriculture. Today, these rural establishments have highly developed facilities, producing plastics, irrigation systems, metal products and even computer components; 60% of the output is exported.

David Ben Gurion, the Nation's First Prime Minister
Featured on Israeli Currency

War & Peace

In 1956, Egypt nationalised the Suez Canal, creating a new conflict – France and Great Britain versus Egypt. It was the start of a second war with Israel, during which Israel occupied the entire Sinai Peninsula. As a result of American pressure, the peninsula was returned to Egypt in 1957. Still, no peace agreement was signed. In 1958, however, an international agreement confirmed that the Gulf of Aqaba was an international waterway, through which Israeli ships had the right of passage. In 1965, a new harbour was built at Eilat.

A third war against Israel began to brew in 1967, with the re-establishment of the Arab High Command, a joint effort of Iraq, Syria, and the United Arab Republic (UAR) – as Egypt was called at the time. On May 19 – at the request of the UAR's President Nasser – the United Nations began withdrawing its peace-keeping forces from the Gaza Strip, a stretch of land which the United Nations had allocated to the Palestinians, but which was controlled by Egypt since 1948.

Despite the accord confirming that the Gulf of Aqaba was an international waterway, on May 22, 1967, the UAR blocked the Straits of Tiran, preventing all Israeli cargo from reaching or leaving Eilat, Israel's only port on the Red Sea. That same day, Israeli Prime Minister Eshkol publicly declared to Cairo and Damascus that Israel had no desire to challenge them. On June 5, Eshkol sent a communication to Jordan's King Hussein:

> We shall not initiate any action whatsoever against Jordan. However, should Jordan open hostilities we shall react with all our might (Mann, 1973, p. 185).

Israel's General Moshe Dayan had already declared that a threat of invasion from Jordan would be "a move which would oblige the Israel Army to capture the West Bank of the river Jordan (Dayan, 1966, p. 36)."

That which came to be known as the Six-Day War broke out on June 5, 1967. In six days, Israel occupied the Gaza Strip, the West Bank, and the Golan Heights. On June 5, Israeli forces cut off the Gaza Strip from Egypt; later that day, Jordan opened a second front, with fighting in Jerusalem.

On June 6, the Israelis penetrated the West Bank; that same day, the United Nations Security Council approved a cease-fire resolution. On June 7, Jordan accepted the United Nations cease-fire and on the Egyptian front Israeli troops occupied Sharm el Sheikh, thereby putting to an end the blockade of the Gulf of Aqaba.

General Moshe Dayan

Under the command of General Moshe Dayan, the Israelis reached the Suez Canal on June 8, 1967, and this ended the war with Egypt. During the next two days, Israel took control of the Golan Heights, from which the Syrians had been shelling Israeli civilian targets. Israel annexed eastern Jerusalem, thus reuniting the city.

All these areas were integrated into the Israeli economy, but at a significant cost. Over time, this led to higher prices and discontent. By 1970, the situation had become a War of Attrition, along the Suez Canal and in the Sinai. In October 1973, Egypt and Syria attacked Israel in what became the Yom Kippur War. Losses were heavy.

During these turbulent times, taxes were high, in order to pay for a high national defence budget. The Labour Party was in power, and the government was heavily involved in the heavily regulated economy, with powerful unions.

Led by Menachem Begin, the right-wing Likud Party was elected in 1977. On March 26, 1979, Prime Minister Menachem Begin signed a peace treaty with Egypt's President Sadat. Under the terms of this accord, Israel gave the entire Sinai Peninsula to Egypt. In so doing, Israel achieved peace with the largest Arab country.

Despite the peace treaty with Egypt, the Israeli economy was bleak. Inflation increased from 43% in 1977 to 112% in 1979 and up to 445% in 1984, as indicated in Table 8.1.

The over-protected economy was in need of massive restructuring. In response to this situation, in July 1985, the coalition government launched a comprehensive economic stabilisation programme. This emergency measure included a wage freeze, cuts in public spending and a pegging of the national currency to the US dollar. On September 4, 1985, a new currency was introduced. One thousand sheqels became one new sheqel.

During the 1990s, Israel's population grew significantly with the mass immigration of about 700,000 people – during a three-year period – from the Soviet Union. Israel also absorbed 30,000 immigrants from Ethiopia during the early 1990s.

Israel began privatising government-held companies in 1991. The first firm to be privatised was the nation's domestic airline, Arkia.

Prime Minister Menachem Begin

YEAR	INFLATION
1979	112%
1980	133%
1981	101%
1982	132%
1983	191%
1984	445%
1985	185%
1986	20%
1987	16%
1988	16%
1989	21%
1990	18%
1991	19%
1992	9%
1993	11%
1994	12%
1995	10%
1996	10%
1997	7%
1998	9%
1999	3%

Table 8.1 Rates of Inflation

In 1993, Israel and the PLO signed their first accord. The following year, it was agreed to allow free movement of goods and services between Israel, the West Bank and the Gaza Strip. In 1994, Israel and Jordan signed their peace agreement; at the Casablanca Conference, the Arab boycott of Israel crumbled. Fast-growing markets opened up to Israel, while foreign investment rushed in. Currency controls were eliminated in May 1998. As less was being spent on defence, more capital was available for R & D in technology. By the year 2000, *Wired* had ranked Israel as the fourth most influential high-tech hub in the world, after Silicon Valley, Boston, and Stockholm-Kista.

In a historic move, on May 26, 2000, Israel was invited to join the Western Europe and Others Group (WEOG) of the United Nations. This made the country eligible for nomination to several committees, including the Security Council. Consensus was secured by all 26 member-nations for Israel to join Canada, the United States, Australia, New Zealand, and western European countries in this grouping.

Research Achievements

According to *Israel, A Scientific Profile,* compiled by Leora Frucht-Eren and published by the British Council, Israeli researchers have been responsible for several major contributions, including the following: discovery of a bacterium that is toxic only to mosquito larvae, and adopted by the World Health Organisation to control malaria; the first demonstration of the effectiveness of deprenyl in treating Parkinson's Disease; the first demonstration of the clinical diagnosis of aminocentesis, used to identify abnormalities in a fetus; invention of affinity chromatography; design of an instrument to scan and sort cells, to detect cancer at an early stage; design of a strategy to fight parasitic weeds, which has already saved crops in Africa and the Middle East; design of an encoding technology for protecting computer-generated data, used in smart-cards; crystallisation of the ribosome; and revelation of the 3-dimensional structure of acetylcholinesterase, the enzyme responsible for nerve impulses.

As well, Israeli researchers have developed the following: a drug for Alzheimer patients, currently being tested in North America; a new method of transplanting bone marrow from non-compatible donors; a paediatric heart surgery technique; lithium substitutes for psychiatric use; a protein to treat chronic hepatitis and herpes; a medical procedure to treat earthquake victims crushed under rubble; a method to heal shattered bones; and a drug to control multiple sclerosis.

Women & Enterprise

Women in Israel – Arab as well as Jewish – were the first in the Middle East to obtain the right to vote. The role of women in Israel subsequently changed more rapidly than was the case in neighbouring countries. The *kibbutz* movement contributed to this, inviting men and women to participate equally in various jobs, on a rotational basis.

Defence considerations also emancipated the women in Israel. Since boys and girls were sent to the army, both men and women came back with a variety of skills, *i.e.*, assets to be used in the non-military economy.

While mainstream women in Israel experienced emancipation, Bedouin men still expected their women to fulfil traditional roles; for instance, women continued to be responsible for sewing and repairing tents.

©2000 by Leo Paul Dana
Ethiopian Women Preparing to Immigrate to Israel

In Bedouin society, the home is still the woman's responsibility. Women make pillows and mattresses. As well, they cook and clean and are expected to bear many children, to care for them, and even to arrange marriages. Women also fetch water when necessary and they harvest dates, grain and olives.

In an attempt to increase entrepreneurship among minorities in Israel, the American Jewish Joint Distribution Committee, Inc. (JDC) initiated a special entrepreneurship and small business programme. June 1993 marked the launch of the "First Entrepreneurship Course in the Arab Sector." As well, the JDC launched an entrepreneurship course for single mothers.

Traditional Spinning

Business Incentives in Israel

While Israel has an advanced and efficient infrastructure, making it a desirable location for business, the government adds to this by having a very positive attitude toward foreign investment; foreigners may participate in all sectors of the economy, except those concerning national defence. The Investment Promotion Centre, at the Ministry of Industry and Trade, is a full-service, "one-stop shop" providing information and contacts for firms considering expansion to Israel. To enhance matters, Israel offers tax holidays, tax allowances, tax reductions, and accelerated rates of depreciation.

With more than 80 venture capital firms in Israel, finance is no longer a problematic issue. Furthermore, special financial incentives are offered to industries that contribute to employment and to exports.

The state offers tax-free investment grants, and a variety of R & D grants. Among these are R & D grants for the development of innovative products (50% of approved expenditures) and R & D grants for new ventures (66% of approved expenditures). In addition, assistance is available to train employees and to reduce the cost of rent. As well, the government provides market research grants and subsidies toward the preparation of business plans. The Marketing Encouragement Fund, for instance, gives financial support to enterprises seeking to enlarge their international marketing efforts.

Bi-national funds are also available in Israel. These include the Singapore Israel Industrial Research and Development Fund.

Complementing the many grants, loans are also readily available. There are several loan funds in Israel, involving $150 million. These include government loan funds, philanthropic loan funds, and private loan funds, as described in detail by Dana (1999c).

In 2000, the Global Entrepreneurship Monitor ranked Israel third in the world in entrepreneurial activity. Entrepreneurs launching enterprises – with up to fifty employees – can further benefit from bank loans guaranteed by the Ministry of Industry and Trade. Small dealers – with a limited turnover – are exempt from collecting VAT.

Bank Leumi Providing Loans to Entrepreneurs

Foreign investors are attracted to Israel's highly educated and motivated workforce and the industrial parks wherein technology is highly concentrated. The Ministry of Industry of Trade supports 26 technological incubators. In 1999, Israel received $7.5 billion in foreign investments, and investment in Israeli companies more than quadrupled in one year.

Israel's free port zones are also attractive; firms can benefit from free port zones in Haifa and Ashdod, on the Mediterranean Sea, and Eilat, on the Red Sea. Goods imported into Eilat, for local use, are VAT-exempt.

Israel is the only country to have free trade agreements with Canada, the European Union, Turkey, and the United States. On March 6, 2000, Israel signed a free trade agreement with Mexico. Israel also has preferential customs agreements and double taxation agreements with other countries. Williams and Dana (forthcoming) elaborate on business opportunities in Israel.

©2000 by Leo Paul Dana

The King David Hotel, Jerusalem

Toward the Future

Until recently, economic development in Israel was hindered by the need for heavy defence expenditures. Israel could not fully benefit from its potential. With peace in the air, it will be increasingly possible to refocus efforts on the economy. International agencies have already been upgrading their financial and business rankings of Israel. Privatisation has created opportunities for a broad range of investors, including those interested in banks and those focused on industry. While financial investment is being prompted by opportunities in local capital markets, industrial investment is being attracted to the high level of technological skills available in Israel. Among successful investors are AT&T, Intel, IBM, Motorola, and Microsoft.

© 2000 by Leo Paul Dana

Foreign Investor Since 1831

A favourable environment for enterprise – coupled with a highly educated workforce and free trade agreements – can only enhance the state of the economy in Israel. It can safely be assumed that peace with its neighbours will open up new markets for Israeli products. Peace will also enable Israelis to sub-contract to enterprises in countries where wages are lower. This will be beneficial in at least two ways. Firstly, this will create employment in neighbouring countries, enhancing the buying power of people who will then be in a better position to purchase Israeli products. As well, producing in low-cost environments will allow for Israeli products to become increasingly competitive in world markets; lower costs can lead to lower prices, which in turn lead to more demand, allowing for greater opportunities of scale, and further reductions in cost.

During its first 50 years of independence, the State of Israel transformed itself from a poor, agriculturally-based country to a world leader in innovation and technology development. Inbound foreign investment in Israel rose from a mere $24 million in 1994, to $1.2 billion in 1998. During its fiftieth year of existence, Israel exported software amounting to $1.5 billion. In 1999, the number of mobile phone service subscriptions surpassed the number of land-based subscriptions in Israel.

Israel has an impressive number of engineers per capita. While the United States has 8 engineers per 1,000 workers, and Japan has 7.5, Israel has 14 qualified engineers per 1,000 workers. While the nation is host to the Digital Equipment Corporation, IBM, Intel, Microsoft, Motorola and National Semiconductors, local new ventures dominate its export-oriented high-tech industry. The economy of Israel is being led by scientific and industrial R & D. High-tech products and services account for three-quarters of exports. This country is headed to become an economic superpower.

Chapter 9

The Hashemite Kingdom of Jordan

Introduction

Jordan covers an area of 89,300 square kilometres. Its neighbours are Iraq, Israel, Saudi Arabia, and Syria. Arabic is the official language.

During most of its history since independence, Jordan was beset by economic difficulties. Until 1948, most of the nation's trade was carried out with its British neighbour to the west; after Israel's independence, the Arab boycott stopped this otherwise fruitful trade.

Outside the Dead Sea, Jordan has few natural resources; however, peace with Israel has made possible the joint development of industry and of the Dead Sea – including the extraction of potassium salts for fertiliser.

> *Our most important natural resource is expertise.*
> – Labour Minister Jawad al-Anani

Historical Overview

Present-day Jordan was formerly ruled by the Greeks, the Romans, and the Byzantines. Between about 500 BC and 200 AD, this land was home to the Aramaic-speaking Nabataeans – business-minded, pre-Islamic Arabs who were prosperous traders; when they were threatened by their enemies, they would dissuade the invaders by explaining that fighting was bad for business.

143

Situated on the cross-roads of major caravan routes linking Egypt, Arabia, and Mesopotamia, the Nabataean capital – Petra – was a hub of international trade. Here, ivory arrived from Africa, and silk from China, as well as incense from Yemen. Petra was the central storage and dispatch centre. From here, it was a month-long trip to Yemen and no other people braved the voyage; the Nabataeans hence had the monopoly on the incense trade. Herod's troops came to Petra and asked to be shown the route to Yemen, but none survived the journey.

The Nabataeans also pioneered petroleum exports. Their camel caravans trekked across the desert, carrying bitumen from the Dead Sea to Gaza and there the cargoes were transferred for shipping to Egypt.

During the Byzantine period – from 324 to 632 AD – Jordanian entrepreneurs prospered by selling provisions to travelling caravans, which linked the Mediterranean with the Far East.

During the 7th century, Muslim Arabs conquered the territory. Then came almost a century of rule by the Crusaders, who were defeated by Salah el Din, in 1187. The Mamelukes then ruled until the arrival of the Ottomans, during the early 16th century. In response to the disloyalty expressed by Bedouins, Sultan Abdul Hamid II decided it would be wise to relocate loyal Ottoman subjects to the Middle East. His new policy, in 1878, exempted migrants to Transjordan from twelve years of taxes, and this encouraged Circassians to move to the land east of the Jordan River. Agricultural and animal herding allowed the population to be self-sufficient.

During the Great War of 1914 – the First World War – Colonel T. E. Lawrence, also known as Lawrence of Arabia, promised the Arabs an independent kingdom, in exchange for assistance in liberating Palestine from the Ottoman Empire. Victorious Britain subsequently divided the territory it conquered from the Ottomans. While the coastal area – west of the Jordan River – would retain the name British Palestine, the Emirate of Transjordan was created on the East Bank. Both territories remained under British mandate.

In 1921, Abdullah ibn Hussein – brother of Arab Prince Faisal who established the government in Syria – was appointed the emir of the new emirate; this entity was a self-governing territory under British mandate. Amman – known by the Romans as Philadelphia – became its capital. Thousands of people began to work for the state. When Transjordan became a kingdom, in 1946, the British made Abdullah its monarch. Transjordan enjoyed a fine friendship with Britain, which continued to subsidise its economy.

When Arab armies invaded Israel, in 1948, radio stations in neighbouring countries advised Palestinians to leave their homes "because Arab cannons would not be able to distinguish between Jews and Arabs, when reducing the country to cinders." The well-to-do *effendis* went abroad, and half a million came to Transjordan. This created economic problems.

In 1949, the country was re-named the Hashemite Kingdom of Jordan, and the West Bank (of the Jordan River) was annexed in 1950.

When King Abdullah was assassinated, in 1951, his son Talal was allowed to rule – but only for a few months, after which he was deposed on the grounds of mental illness. Talal's son, Hussein ibn Talal succeeded him.

Often, industrialisation leads to urbanisation. In Jordan, urbanisation was spurred by immigration, and until the 1950s, industrialisation was relatively slow, allowing merchants and agents for foreign firms to dominate markets. Then, urbanisation prompted industrialisation. While the government operated large-scale industries, the small enterprise sector was limited, as industrial entrepreneurs were few. There was little investment in manufacturing.

In 1956, the Sinai Campaign led Jordan to break its ties with London – an expensive decision, as this meant foregoing $36 million a year in subsidies. Fearing that communism would replace British influence, the United States provided economic assistance when England stopped doing so. In 1958, Jordan joined Iraq to create the Arab Federal State, but this entity was demised after Iraq became its own republic, in July 1958.

In 1960, Jordan offered citizenship to all Arab refugees applying for it. The population of Jordan subsequently swelled with Palestinians. In 1965, King Hussein traded land with Saudi Arabia, thereby extending the Jordanian shoreline along the Gulf of Aqaba. This would allow development of Jordan's port city.

On June 5, 1967, Jordan joined in the Six-Day War against Israel. In a counterattack by the Israelis, on June 6, Jordan lost the West Bank, which it had annexed seventeen years earlier. The next day, Jordan gave up East Jerusalem and accepted a United Nations cease-fire.

Following the Six-Day War, Jordan's industrial production dropped by a fifth. The West Bank had produced 70% of Jordan's fruits.

In 1970, Palestinian guerrillas clashed with the Jordanian army, and the following year, the prime minister of Jordan was assassinated by Palestinians in Cairo.

When Jordan did away with compulsory military service, in 1991, it was the first Arab country to do so. Less military expenditure meant more funding available for economic development.

   Peace with Israel – signed in 1994 – ushered in a new era of prosperity for Jordan. The agreement opened up a new market for Jordanian products, while giving a greater range of products to Jordanian consumers. Prior to the peace agreement, tourism has been growing at an annual rate of 1%; since then, the tourism sector has been growing by as much as 18% a year.

   King Hussein died on February 7, 1999, a day after his eldest son – Abdullah ibn Al-Hussein al Hashemi – was sworn in as regent.

Agriculture

Outside shops selling green almonds, vine-leaves and mint, the scent of rose water emanates from rows of micro-scale confectioneries making *konafeh* and selling fresh *bassboussah* for 10 *ersh* (under 14 cents). Jordanians enjoy fresh and tasty foods.

© 2000 by Leo Paul Dana

Making *Konafeh* During Ramadan

© 2000 by Leo Paul Dana

Sweet Shop in Amman

In spite of its semi-arid climate, the fertile Jordan Valley produces three harvests a year; this includes citrus fruits, bananas, melons, and vegetables. The central highlands, which receive more rain, provide cereal grains as well as fruits and vegetables. Much Jordanian produce is exported.

In accordance with the Investment Promotion Law, agricultural projects benefit from exemptions from customs duties, social service contributions and income tax. Flexible loans are available from specialised credit institutions.

Sustainable Development

The Badia region of Jordan is an arid zone, which has tremendous potential in terms of providing electricity. The very intense sun and desert winds are ideal for the production of non-pollutant, renewable energy. Furthermore, ground water makes possible the cultivation of land, while the landscape could attract tourism.

In May 1992, the Royal Geographic Society of the United Kingdom launched a joint development programme with the Jordanian Secretariat of the Higher Council of Science & Technology and the Centre for Overseas Research & Development of Durham University. Known as the Jordan Badia Research & Development Programme, its objective was specified as the sustainable development of the desertified Badia environment. The programme was housed in the former complex of the H5 pumping station, along the Karuk-Haifa pipeline.

Improving the Infrastructure

Jordan has significantly improved its infrastructure during the past decade. Beginning in 1993, the telecom policy evolved into the National Telecommunications Programme, raising the penetration ratio of phone lines. The Telecommunications Corporation was commercialised and restructured into the Jordan Telecom Company, which now operates three satellite earth stations. The Telecom Regulatory Commission was also established, to provide a transparent and fair competitive environment for service companies.

Maritime transport and railway companies benefit from full duty exemptions on fixed assets. In addition, they are entitled to a 75% exemption on income tax and the same on social services tax.

Business Incentives in Jordan

Jordan has been creating an attractive environment for enterprise, allowing the free flow of capital and profits. To promote investment, tax rates have been reduced and capital gains and dividends are exempt from tax. Hotels, hospitals, industrial firms and mining enterprises pay income tax at the rate of 15%. Insurance companies and banks pay 35%. All others are taxed at the rate of 25%.

© 2000 by Leo Paul Dana

The Jordan Islamic Bank

Investment Law N°16 of 1995 – published in the *Official Gazette*, Issue 4075, October 16, 1995 – superseded the Encouragement of Investment Law N°11, of 1987, and the Law Regulating Arab and Foreign Investments N°27, of 1992. The new legislation led to the creation of the Investment Promotion Corporation (IPC), an independent legal entity, responsible for marketing Jordan internationally. The IPC creates links between Jordanian firms and counterparts abroad; it assists investors and serves as liaison with the government. Among its services, it identifies opportunities for investments; it facilitates the registration and licensing of investments; and it tabulates data and technical information, for distribution to interested parties.

In 1999, the IPC opened the Investor Reception Centre, in the North Terminal of Queen Alia International Airport, in Amman. The centre welcomes prospective investors and facilitates immigration procedures. Representatives are available to help individuals plan their itinerary. On site, there are fax and Internet facilities for use by business people. The centre also provides a database on business and industry in Jordan, along with a repository of joint venture and other investment opportunities.

To enhance its role as a hub of commerce, Jordan has created Free Zones for manufacturing and storage of transient goods. Products, in such zones, are duty-exempt. Salaries of foreign employees in Free Zones are exempted from income tax and social service payments.

The first public Free Zones was established in Aqaba. There are also private Free Zones in Aqaba, Qweira, and Shidieh.

The Jordan Industrial Estates Corporation provides industry parks with vocational training centres. Firms operating in these parks are permanently exempted from real estate taxes. The Sahab Estate is 3 kilometres from Amman; its 250 hectares (625 acres) accommodate about 350 firms, employing 14,000 persons. Further north is the smaller Al Hassan Industrial Estate; in 1998, the United States designated this estate as the world's first Qualifying Industrial Zone (QIZ). The Gateway Project Company's Jordan Valley Free Zone was designated as the second QIZ.

A firm with a qualifying product – produced in a QIZ – has duty-free access to the United States, and no quotas on production. In addition, fixed assets for production enter Jordan free of duty. Firms are entitled to total exemptions from income tax and social contributions, when operating in a QIZ.

Amman Street Scene

To qualify for QIZ incentives, at least 35% of a product's appraised value must have QIZ content, with one of five options:

1. If at least 8% of a product's value originates in Israel, and 11.7% in a Jordanian QIZ, then the product is qualifies for QIZ privileges provided that the remaining value added to reach 35% comes from any of the following: Israel, a Jordanian QIZ, Palestinian territories, or the United States. In the case of high-tech products, these qualify if at least 7% of the value originates in Israel, and 11.7% in a Jordanian QIZ, provided that the remaining value added to reach 35% comes from any of the following: Israel, a Jordanian QIZ, Palestinian territories, or the United States.

2. A product qualifies for QIZ incentives when produced by joint Israeli-Jordanian efforts in which Israeli and Jordanian manufacturers each maintain a minimum of 20% of total production costs. Raw materials, design, wages, salaries, research and development, all count toward production costs.

3. A product may qualify for QIZ incentives if it is the result of a joint Israeli-Jordanian effort in which Israelis provide at least 20% of the total production cost, while 11.7% of the content originates in a Jordanian QIZ.
4. A product may qualify for QIZ incentives if it is the result of a joint Israeli-Jordanian effort in which Jordanians provides at least 20% of the total production cost, while a minimum of 8% of the content comes from Israel.
5. A high-tech product may qualify for QIZ incentives if it is the result of a joint Israeli-Jordanian effort in which Jordanians provides at least 20% of the total production cost, while a minimum of 7% of the content comes from Israel.

Land and buildings in Qualifying Industrial Zones may be leased or purchased, via the Industrial Estates Corporation. There is no restriction on project ownership, and profits may be fully repatriated tax-free.

Organisations, which promote business in Jordan, include: the Amman Chamber of Commerce; the Amman Chamber of Industry; the Amman World Trade Centre; the Federation of Jordanian Chambers of Commerce; the Jordanian Businessmen Association; the Jordanian Export Development and Commercial Centres Corporation; the Jordanian National Committee of the International Chamber of Commerce; and the Jordan Trade Association.

The Small Business Sector

Entrepreneurs in Jordan are likely to have had a self-employed father. Most industrialists in Jordan have college degrees; typically, they have entered industry relatively late in life. Yet, their industrial enterprises usually employ fewer than five people.

A large proportion of entrepreneurs in Jordan, produce mostly-custom-made products, made to order. Few individuals are keen to take the risk and to make something that may not sell.

To assist the small business sector, the Queen Alia Jordan Social Fund allocated funds to teach people to train entrepreneurs. The name of the fund was later changed to the Jordanian Hashemite Fund for Human Development.

In conjunction with the International Labour Organisation, the Amman Chamber of Industry developed a seminar to help existing entrepreneurs. As well, the Jordan Institute of Management – an autonomous division of the Industrial Development Bank – has been training entrepreneurs and potential entrepreneurs.

In co-operation with the United Nations Industrial Development Organisation (UNIDO), the Ministry of Industry has been preparing profiles of project opportunities suitable for small-scale entrepreneurs. The same ministry has also been working on developing micro-enterprise in remote areas; this has project has been assisted by the German Agency for Technical Co-operation.

© 2000 by Leo Paul Dana

Amman Bustling with Small Business

Traditional Market in Jordan

Special financial assistance has also been made available to entrepreneurs. The Development & Employment Fund was established, to support self-employment projects. As well, the Small-Scale Industries & Handicrafts Fund – operated by the Industrial Development Bank – has been directing loans to enterprises with fewer than five employees.

Women in Jordan

The Jordanian constitution gives women equal rights as men, with regard to work. The National Charter gives women equal opportunities as men, in education, training, and employment. Women also get the same paid leave-of-absence for the purpose of *haj* – pilgrimage.

The Business & Professional Women's Club encourages women to become entrepreneurs, and it provides assistance to women in business. The Noor Al-Hussein Foundation – in co-operation with the General Federation of Jordanian Women and with funding from the United Nations Population Fund – initiated a Women & Development Programme to encourage entrepreneurship among Jordanian women.

Also, the Jordan River Foundation initiated income generation projects for women, including weaving and embroidery. The foundation supports micro and small enterprises, mostly for women. Focus is on sustainable micro-finance programmes for owners of micro-enterprises – mostly women, who cannot access commercial banks.

Yet, local culture views the economic independence of women as disruptive of family life. Therefore, the participation of women, in the labour force, is still low. Furthermore, unemployment is higher among women than it is among men. When asked about this, employers explained to the author that since the labour law dictates a policy of equal pay for equal work, it therefore makes economic sense to hire men rather than women. "Women get paid leave-of-absence in the case of childbirth – so it is better not to hire them."

Many women are self-employed, and official statistics are misleading, as they do not reflect those working from their home. It is common for village women to produce traditional handicrafts – including embroidered dresses and pillowcases – at their place of residence.

In the formal sector, as well, women are concentrated in the textile industry. They are also clustered in leatherworks, chemical industries, and service industries including banking, tourism and hospitality.

Data obtained from the Development & Employment Fund indicate that credits have been given to women in a variety of domains. Most of these entrepreneurs had sewing and knitting enterprises. Others were in goat-raising, poultry-raising, bee-keeping, dairy-processing and patisseries.

Toward the Future

Jordanian policy may be described as forward-looking. The Companies Law states that a public shareholding company must allocate at least 1% of its annual net profits toward supporting vocational training and scientific research. The presence of a skilled workforce, coupled with competitive wages, gives Jordan a competitive advantage in world markets. Although the concept of minimum wage was recently introduced, in Jordan, salaries are still low enough to make Jordanian industry very competitive.

Since the peace agreement with Israel, Jordan has also benefited from Israeli technology and access to the Israeli market. In addition, the QIZ concept gives Jordanian firms a great advantage, enabling further cost reductions thanks to economies of scale.

In November 1999, King Abdullah ibn Hussein launched a push for socio-economic and fiscal reforms, including modernisation and accelerated privatisation. In January 2000, at the World Economic Forum in Davos, he reaffirmed his commitment to the growth of the private sector.

Given the high educational level of Jordanian entrepreneurs, and the low wages expected by employees, Jordanian firms have a comparative advantage, in regional and in world markets. Jordan's market-oriented economy, coupled with a stable political environment, government incentives and a world-class infrastructure, suggest that Jordan will have very fruitful economic times ahead.

©2000 by Leo Paul Dana

Co-operation with Israel Contributing to Development & Prosperity

Chapter 10

The Republic of Lebanon

Blessed with beauty, rich in antiquity and prosperous from commerce...
– Ellis & Mobley (1970)

Introduction

Covering 10,425 square kilometres, Lebanon lies between Israel, Syria and the Mediterranean Sea. The name Lebanon is said to be derived from *leben* – Aramaic for whiteness.

Since ancient times, commerce has been the lifeline of this land and its people. The Phoenicians – outstanding seafarers, explorers and traders – built ships from cedar trees of Lebanon. From the Lebanese coast, the Phoenicians set sail to establish trading colonies along the northern shoreline of Africa, as well as in Malta, Sardinia, Sicily, and Spain.

After the fall of the Ottomans, Lebanon enjoyed a period of rapid industrialisation. Unlike its neighbours, where the state was the major economic player, it was private enterprise that developed Lebanon. The nation came to be known as the Switzerland of the Middle East. Its capital, Beirut – with the largest gold market between Tangiers and Bombay – was nicknamed the Paris of the Middle East. Entrepreneurship – dominated by traders – characterised the country, though not necessarily the industrial sector (Sayigh, 1962).

With 220 kilometres of shoreline along the Mediterranean Sea, geographic location is an important asset for Lebanon. Beirut is a major port for goods being sent to or from Syria and points east. An entrepreneurial culture is very vibrant here, and post-war reconstruction is progressing well. Banking – with strict secrecy – is a major industry in Lebanon. Almost 100 banks operate here with great efficiency.

Historical Overview

Just north of today's Beirut, the Canaanite city of Byblos – known today as Jebeil – is among the oldest continuously inhabited settlements in the world. It was an important trading hub for Semites and for Egyptians. During a period of five centuries, Byblos was the most important town of the Eastern Mediterranean, until it was eclipsed by the Phoenician towns of Sidon and Tyre, where the world's first phonetic alphabet was introduced. Aramaic later replaced Phoenician as the regional language.

The strategic location of Lebanon made it the desire of many. Persia, Assyria, Babylonia, Egypt and Greece all fought to control this land. It fell under Roman rule in 64 BC. Maronite Christianity – an Eastern sect but with allegiance to the pope – came from Syria. When Islam arrived from the east, most Lebanese Christians kept their faith.

During the 11th century, a Druze community was established in Lebanon. To this day, the Druze people comprise a distinct ethnic group and they tend not to mingle with outsiders. They trace their origins to Darazi and Hamza ibn Ali, two missionaries whom Fatimid caliph al-Hakim encouraged to spread the Ismaili faith in Lebanon. During the 11th century, this developed into a new religion, with its own scripture, the *Risail al-Hikma* – the Book of Wisdom. Druze leaders replaced the Muslim Sharia with their own law, and they developed their own traditions. The Druze people abstain from polygamy, and they allow women to pray with men during services. Wise elders – men – who lead an exemplary life, wear a white turban.

By the 12th century, the region was under Christian Crusader rule. The Mamelukes took over during the 13th century.

The Ottomans controlled Lebanon from the 16th century until the first world war. During the 1830s, a new Christian commercial bourgeoisie arose in Beirut, becoming a prosperous and educated Arabic-speaking middle class. Concern by these Christians, about the Druze community in Lebanon, prompted England and France to pressure the Ottomans into establishing a government which would favour Christians. By 1864, France and Britain convinced the Ottomans to establish a semi-autonomous Christian province within the empire. The Republic of Mount Lebanon – officially ruled by a *mutessariff* (governor general) appointed by the Ottoman sultan – was home to Druze communities as well as to Maronites and Shi'ites. (The Shi'ites revere Mohammed's son-in-law, Ali.) Free from Ottoman taxes, the Lebanese flourished with commerce.

With the downfall of the Ottoman Empire, the Ottoman currency was replaced by a Sterling-based Egyptian currency, issued by a private British institution, the National Bank of Egypt.

Modern-day Lebanon was formed in 1920, from five Ottoman districts, which the League of Nations gave to France. In 1924, Lebanon and Syria signed a convention with the *Banque de Syrie*. The bank – renamed *Banque de Syrie et du Liban* – became the official bank of the Levant states under French mandate. According to the convention, the *Banque de Syrie et du Liban* was granted the exclusive right to issue currency – redeemable in Paris or Marseilles – for Lebanon and Syria, until 1939.

© 2000 by Leo Paul Dana

The Ottoman Bank – Affiliate and Shareholder of the *Banque de Syrie*

In 1937, however, a new convention extended the bank's right to issue Lebanese pounds – separate from the Syrian currency – until 1964. The Lebanese pound – locally known as the lira – was pegged to the French franc, until 1941, when the French mandate was withdrawn and the Lebanese lira was linked to the Sterling.

During the war, the Vichy government administered Lebanon. The National Pact of 1943 was designed to assure the dominance of Christians in Lebanon.

Allied forces invaded in 1945. Lebanon became independent and in 1949, the Monetary Law asserted the independence of Lebanon's monetary system.

© 2000 by Leo Paul Dana

Lebanon Offered a Taste of the West

On August 1, 1963, the Code of Money and Credit created a new central bank, the *Banque du Liban*. It began operations on April 1, 1964, and Lebanon became the financial capital of the Eastern Mediterranean.

In 1975, 4% of the Lebanese population controlled 32% of the nation's wealth. Civil war erupted in April 1975, and lasted until October 1990. The war destroyed much infrastructure and led to an exodus of people along with a flight of capital. Inflation was rampant during the war, reaching 487% in 1987. Simultaneously, the Lebanese currency tumbled, from 3 pounds per dollar in 1975, to 2,000 per dollar in 1992. Under the leadership of Prime Minister Rafiq Hariri – appointed in October 1992 – the government focused on restraining its budget, stabilising its currency, reconstructing the infrastructure, and attracting foreign capital, rebuilding Lebanon as an international financial centre.

Encouraging Business

Lebanon has a long history of encouraging private enterprise. The Association of Lebanese Industrialists was established in 1943. It is a private organisation, which provides services to members, and also lobbies at the governmental level. Representing three quarters of the capital invested in Lebanese industry, the organisation has considerable political clout. The association is directly represented in several decision-making entities, including: the Board of Directors of the Lebanese Norms and Standards Organisation; the Customs Assessment Committees; the Economic Advisory Committee to the Prime Minister; the High Council for Professional and Vocational Education; and the Official Committee on Trade Agreements.

The highest authority of the Association of Lebanese Industrialists is its General Assembly, which consists of all duly registered members in good standing. The Board of Directors – elected by the General Assembly – functions through four bodies:

1. The Bureau is the executive steering committee of the Board. This committee consists of individuals elected by the Board, from its members. These include the President, Vice-Presidents, and Controllers.
2. The Specialised Committees include members of the General Assembly as well as members of the Board.
3. The Sectoral Council groups manufacturers according to their sectors. It is specialised, in that it focuses on particular sectors.

4. Given the different issues relevant in different regions of Lebanon, the Geographic Council focuses on special needs of members in particular regions.

Through the above, the Association of Lebanese Industrialists provides a variety of services to its members. It provides legal advice, vocational training, technical education, and sales promotion of locally-manufactured products. It also renders services such as the certification of invoices.

At the international level, the Association of Lebanese Industrialists is represented at the International Labour Organisation, and the National Committee of the United Nations Industrial Development Organisation. The association participates in the formulation of international legislation, secures assistance for vocational training programmes, and secures industrial credit facilities.

Since 1955, the *Banque du Credit Agricole, Industriel et Foncier* has been lending funds to assist entrepreneurs in farm-related activities. Between 1963 and 1998, the *Banque Nationale du Développement Industriel et Touristique* provided finance to Lebanese industrialists.

© 2000 by Leo Paul Dana

Lebanon Produces Excellent Olives

Another organisation, which assists entrepreneurs, is the *Association d'Entraide Professionnelle* (AEP) established in October 1984, to contribute to socio-economic development. This is a non-profit foundation, created with the support of Lebanese businessmen, interested in social issues, and Lebanese social workers aware of the importance of the economic factor in social rehabilitation. The objective of the organisation is to sustain small project holders, by giving them access to micro-credit and prompting them to become more responsible and active participants in their environment. In consideration of the fact that small-scale enterprises and family businesses, in Lebanon, have had difficulty obtaining credit from banks, the AEP made available loan funds, which are lent for terms of short to medium duration. Priority is given to applicants who cannot obtain financing from banks; support families; have productive, realistic and profitable business plans; have relevant experience; and have guarantees. The ceiling per loan is approximately $5,000.

The government has also been contributing to business, by creating conducive conditions for business. In 1993, the government embarked on a $12 billion programme – Horizon 2000 – aimed at doubling the per capita GDP by 2002. The result has been a business-friendly environment. Investors in Lebanon can benefit from free trade and four tax-exempt industrial zones. The Investment Development Authority of Lebanon provides investors with access to information, advice on legal requirements, and advice on financing. Corporate tax is limited to 15%.

In 1994, Lebanon became the first Arabic-speaking country to tap into the Eurobond market. The absence of capital gains tax, coupled with a 5% withholding tax, encouraged the inflow of capital.

The Investment Development Authority of Lebanon – established by decree of the Council of Ministers in 1994 – became fully operational in 1995. Its primary function is to attract private capital to Lebanon. Its projects have included a $30 million project to raise dairy cattle and a $20 million project to expand a poultry operation.

Also assisting the agro-food industry is the Green Plan, an autonomous public authority for agricultural development in Lebanon. Established by the government, it is funded by the state, and it operates under the tutelage of the Ministry of Agriculture. Its purpose is to assist farmers and to re-terrace hillsides. With headquarters in Beirut, and eight regional offices, the Green Plan employs 200 people, over half of which are technical experts, such as engineers and surveyors.

The Green Plan has a number of on-going projects. One is the Irrigation Rehabilitation & Modernisation Project. Another is the Agriculture Infrastructure Development Project. The latter – an ongoing project initiated in 1996 – is aimed at developing the nation's agricultural infrastructure by the year 2002. Its mandate is to facilitate an increase in food production along with an improvement in the standard of living of farmers.

© 2000 by Leo Paul Dana

Lebanon Produces High-quality Figs

The Ministry of Agriculture has also been actively encouraging the establishment of agricultural co-operatives and promoting the development of food-processing industries. In addition, the Ministry of Agriculture has been encouraging women to play a visible role in rural development.

Toward the Future

A low income tax schedule and a liberal economic policy are encouraging investment in Lebanon. Furthermore, a government programme – administered by the *Conseil du Développement et de la Reconstruction /* Council for Development and Reconstruction – is aiming to make Beirut an international business centre to compete with Hong Kong and Singapore. State-of-the-art digital technology, fibre-optic cables and a cellular network have already replaced Lebanon's analogue communication system.

Although civil war led to a brain-drain and a flight of capital during the late 20th century, peace is prompting educated Lebanese entrepreneurs to return to Lebanon, bringing with them skills and capital. Lebanon has once again become an international financial centre, and it is poised to become a hub of international business, in the very near future.

Driving Across the Lebanese Border at Rosh Hanikra

Chapter 11

Palestine

Introduction

In November 1988, Yasser Arafat – locally known as Abu Ammar – declared the establishment of the State of Palestine, covering the Gaza Strip and the West Bank (of the Jordan River), collectively referred to – since 1967 – as Occupied Territories. Together, the Gaza Strip and the West Bank cover about 6,000 square kilometres, home to an estimated 2.5 million people. Approximately 4 million Palestinians live outside these areas, and many of these are expected to return, as economic prospects brighten. According to the United Nations Relief and Works Agency, as many as 350,000 Palestinians could come from Lebanon, and another 350,000 from Syria, in addition to 1.4 million from Jordan.

> *Before 1967...we had the land but did not utilise it.*
> *No factories, little trade and no tourism.*
> – Dr. Mohammad A. Sarsour
> General Manager, Beit El-Mal Holdings

After 1967, the Palestinian economy became linked to that of Israel. Between 1968 and 1970, per capita GNP in Gaza rose by 46%.

Until the 1990s, the economy of the Gaza Strip and of the West Bank relied heavily on Israel, and one third of the labour force commuted to Israel for employment, thus contributing more than a quarter of the GNP. Israel remains an important market for Palestinian products; 80% of industrial exports go to Israeli markets, helping in the development of a strong industrial base for Palestinians.

Historical Overview

The Palestinians trace their origins to the Philistines, who lived between the Egyptians to the west and the Israelites to the northeast. Today, the coastal land between Egypt and Israel, along the Mediterranean coast, is referred to as the Gaza Strip, named after its principal city and port, Gaza.

It is believed that Gaza was founded 4,000 years ago, by frankincense traders from Yemen. The walled city overlooked fertile land, which produced almonds, barley, olives and vegetables. While Gaza prospered with trade, its wealth made it the envy of many, and this prompted several invasions. Gaza was ruled by Egyptians, Persians, Babylonians, Greeks, Seleucids, Syrians, Assyrians, Judaeans, Romans, Sejuk Turks, Muslim Arabs and Crusaders. Led by Richard the Lion-Hearted, the Crusaders destroyed Gaza's city walls and built a church, which was later refurbished to become a mosque. Following Crusader rule, Gaza was governed by the Egyptian Mamelukes and then by the Ottoman Empire, Britain, Egypt and Israel.

With the spread of Islam, camel caravans from North Africa passed through Gaza, on their way to Mecca for *haj* – pilgrimage. Traders provided provisions for thousands of pilgrims who stocked up on almonds, apples, barley, corn, dates, figs, lemons, olives, oranges, vegetables, watermelons and wheat.

For centuries, until World War I, Gaza was an important shipping hub for international commerce. As the Ottoman Empire weakened, the prominence of Gaza faded. The British occupied Gaza on November 7, 1917. Having conquered Ottoman Palestine, the British divided it. In 1926, the eastern part became the Emirate of Transjordan – today's Jordan.

In 1947, British Palestine was further partitioned by a United Nations proposal to create two new entities – a Jewish state and an Arab state – side-by-side. According to the United Nations partition plan, Judaea, Samaria and the Gaza Strip would become a Palestinian state upon the termination of the British mandate on May 15, 1948. The Jews accepted the United Nations partition plan, but when they declared the independence of Israel in May 1948, the armies of five Arab nations invaded the Jewish state.

Although provisions had been made for a Palestinian state, Jordan annexed Biblical Judaea and Samaria – collectively known as the West Bank – while Egypt took control of entire Gaza Strip.

© 2000 by Leo Paul Dana

Traditional Transport

Palestinian Arabs – Christians and Muslims – who found themselves within the boundaries of Israel, were given Israeli nationality. Those in the Gaza Strip found themselves ruled by the Egyptians, and those in the West Bank, by the Jordanians. Almost 800,000 Palestinians became refugees; in 1964, the Palestine Liberation Organisation (PLO) was formed, to further their cause.

Until 1967, agriculture was the backbone of the Palestinian economy, whether under Egyptian or Jordanian rule. As an aftermath of the Six-Day War – during which Israel took control of the Gaza Strip and the West Bank – Palestinians from these territories were allowed to seek employment in Israel.

© 2000 by Leo Paul Dana

Dogs Used to Herd Flocks

After 1967, the economy of the Palestinian people shifted away from agriculture, as Palestinians found wages in Israel more attractive than farming in the Gaza Strip or the West Bank. Both Israeli and Jordanian currencies flowed freely in the West Bank. Under Israeli rule, Palestinians spread out beyond the geographic scope of their ancestral lands, and into the Sinai Desert. The sprawling town of Rafah came to include a southern suburb, known as Mukhayim Canada, technically in the Sinai. Its residents typically went to work in Israel, and their children to school in the Gaza Strip. This was so until August 25, 1982, when Israel completed its hand-over of the Sinai to Egypt; the international border then cut through Rafah, as coils of razor wire sliced the city in two, leaving the 4,500 Palestinians of Mukhayim Canada on the Egyptian side of the border. This day came to be known as *youm iswid* – "black day." Thereafter, Mukhayim Canada remained cut off from the Gaza Strip by *El Silik* – the wire. Unable to physically get to work in Israel, 70% of adult men in Mukhayim Canada were idle, and the Egyptians did not allow them to seek employment in Egypt. Only later, Israel provided land and the Government of Canada provided financial support for some families to relocate in the Gaza Strip.

Nevertheless, there remained countless Palestinian refugees in various countries. When, in 1982, Lebanese Christians massacred Palestinians near Beirut, 700,000 Israelis protested the massacre.

Also in 1982, Yair Hirschfeld – a New Zealander born to Austrian parents – began an informal dialogue, which would outshine his career as a history professor at Haifa University; he served as the link between the Israeli government and the PLO.

In 1988, Jordan's King Hussein ceded all territorial claims to the West Bank, to the PLO. That November, Palestine was declared.

© 2000 by Leo Paul Dana

Trilingual Shop Sign in Bethlehem

In 1989, Palestinian businessmen and politicians formed the European Palestinian Chamber of Commerce. This is a non-profit organisation, which assists Palestinian companies exporting to Europe. The organisation provides training, information, and contacts.

During the Gulf War of 1990, Palestinian support for Iraq led to a deterioration of relations between the Palestinians and the West. In July 1991, the Lebanese Army – backed by Syrian forces – forced the PLO to retreat from its positions in southern Lebanon.

On September 13, 1993, the PLO signed a peace agreement with Israel. In accordance with the Israeli-PLO Declaration of Principle, Israel's Prime Minister, Yitzhak Rabin allowed Palestinians self-rule in the Gaza Strip and in Jericho (on the West Bank). Palestinian leadership subsequently moved from Tunisia to the Middle East, and the Palestinian Authority began its administration in May 1994.

In September 1995, Israel agreed to transfer powers and responsibilities from the Israeli Military Government and its Civil Administration to the Palestinian Council. This came to be known as the Oslo 2 Agreement (see Exhibit 11.1). That same month, Yasser Arafat sent greetings of *Shana Tova* to "our cousins the Jews and the Israeli people."

In September 1996, the Expatriates Affairs Department, of the Ministry of Planning and International Co-operation, sponsored a convention for Palestinians living abroad. The emphasis was on encouraging Palestinians working abroad to invest in Gaza and in the West Bank. Ahed Tamini – representing the Ministry of Labour – announced that investors will be allowed to settle in the territories; it was felt that Palestinians should not simply invest money, but also time and effort in managing local firms. A representative of the Ministry of Economy & Trade undertook to facilitate importing.

In October 1998, Israel and the Palestinian Authority signed the Wye Accord. In accordance with the conditions of this agreement, the Palestine National Council voted to remove anti-Israel clauses from the PLO's charter. On May 17, 1999, the Israelis elected Ehud Barak, with a platform calling for regional peace.

The Government of the State of Israel and the Palestine Liberation Organisation (hereafter the PLO) the representative of the Palestinian people;
Within the framework of the Middle East peace process...
Reaffirming their determination to put an end to decades of confrontation...
While recognising mutual legitimate and political rights ...
Recognising that the peace process and the new era it has created ... are irreversible ...
Recognising that the aim of Israel-Palestinian negotiations ... is ...
heading to a permanent settlement ...
Desirous of putting into effect the
Declaration of Principles on Interim Self-Government Arrangements
Signed at Washington DC, on September 13, 1993 ...
Hereby agree as follows:

CHAPTER 1: *Transfer of Authority.* Israel shall transfer powers and responsibilities ... from the Israeli Military Government and its Civil Administration to the Palestinian Council ...

CHAPTER 2: *Land.* The two sides view the West Bank and the Gaza Strip as a single territorial unity, the integrity and status of which will be preserved.

Signed in Washington DC, September 28, 1995

Exhibit 11.1. Excerpt from the Israel-PLO Oslo 2 Agreement

The Environment for Enterprise

The Palestinian Authority is solely responsible for the regulation of all business activities in the Gaza Strip and on the West Bank. However, experts told the author that "the Palestinian regulatory and tax systems are, to say the least, user-unfriendly." The European Commission funded a training programme on the management of government functions. Yet, Palestinians have conveyed to the author that favouritism has been on the rise – unlike the situation as it was when the Gaza Strip and the West Bank were under Israeli administration.

> For 27 years we blamed our poor economy on the Israeli occupation. But in the same time our economy improved. Individual income increased, housing projects every where, and unemployment decreased…Yet we are good of blaming our problems on other people. So if not to blame it on the West, who to blame it on?
> – Dr. Mohammad A. Sarsour
> Quoted in *Palestine Business Report*
> Vol. 1, N° 10, October 1996, p. 18.

Another concern is that business plans are difficult to assemble, given that statistics on local market trends are lacking. To fill the gap, the Economic Statistics Programme – which includes the Industrial Statistics Programme – established the System of Official Statistics for Palestine. Their economic surveys, launched in 1994, include studies on construction, transport and industry, in line with international recommendations specified in the *United Nations Manual for Industrial Statistics*.

One statistic, which is widely known, is that Palestinian firms rely on Israeli buyers for 80% of their industrial exports; about half the raw materials come from Israel.

To attract large-scale foreign investment and to facilitate economies of scale, the Gaza Industrial Zone was established. The World Bank contributed $50 million toward this project.

Until 1996, banks in the Gaza Strip and on the West Bank focused on short-term loans. To fill the need for longer-term investments, the World Bank accepted to enter a joint venture with existing banks, to create the Arab Palestinian Bank for Investment, based in Ramallah, with a liaison office in Gaza. This was a joint project involving the Arab Bank (based in Jordan), the International Finance Corporation (subsidiary of the World Bank), the German Investment and Development Company (DEG), and the Enterprise Investment Company. Among its first concerns was a $23 million project to develop handicraft work.

In 1996, a business centre was established in Ramallah, to promote private enterprise development in Palestine. This was an initiative of the European Union, in association with the Palestinian Authority. With the objective of establishing sustainable export-oriented industrial sectors, cost-sharing support was offered to Palestinian firms to develop their products to internationally competitive standards.

Palestinians nevertheless express concern that their educational background does not reflect the needs of enterprises, either in the Gaza Strip or on the West Bank. It was pointed out, for instance, that the universities in the Gaza Strip – El-Azhar University, Islamic University, Open University and the College of Education – are not enterprise-based. For this reason, recent efforts have been focused on training individuals for enterprise, especially self-employment.

The Small Business Sector

Palestinian businesses tend to be family-owned, and 90% of Palestinian firms have fewer than five workers. Experts argue that the economic environment in the Gaza Strip and in the West Bank is more conducive for the development of small enterprises, rather than multinational investment. To encourage the small business sector, several initiatives have been launched.

© 2000 by Leo Paul Dana

Small-scale Palestinian Bakery

In March 1995, the Development & Planning Department, in Gaza, established the Small and Micro Enterprise Training Programme, providing training courses in a variety of subjects. Initially, courses ranged from 15 to 24 hours in duration. Later, longer courses were introduced. In consideration of the cost involved in bringing in trainers from abroad, it was decided that most courses be taught by local trainers.

Over time, the range of topics was enlarged. Initial offerings included the following courses:

- Accountancy for Small Business
- Business Communications
- Feasibility Study
- Management of Infrastructure
- Micro & Small Enterprise Development
- Start Your Own Business
- Total Quality Management

In 1998, additional topics were introduced: Hotel & Restaurant Management; Management of Small Business; Tourism Marketing and Promotion; Safety & Health; Doing Business by Internet; Accounting for Selling by Instalment; Construction Documentation; Menu Planning & Pricing; Food & Beverage Services; and Tour Programme Management. Each course attracts a symbolic participation fee. Most participants are business owners. Table 11.1 summarises some relevant statistics.

Year	Courses	Total Participants	Typical Class Size
1995	15	368	24
1996	25	565	23
1997	29	495	17
1998	32	445	14
Total	101	1,873	19

Table 11.1 Courses of the Small and Micro Enterprise Training Programme

The Small & Medium Enterprises Development Association in Palestine (SMEDA) was founded in 1998, on the initiative of small business owners and development experts. SMEDA is a non-profit organisation; it is the first organisation of entrepreneurs in the region, owned and operated by business-owners, with the co-operation of the Ministry of Industry. The objectives of SMEDA include:

- To train entrepreneurs;
- To research entrepreneurship and disseminate knowledge;
- To facilitate networking among members;
- To improve the operating environment for small and medium-sized firms;
- To lobby for simplified paperwork requirements and tax concessions;
- To create a culture of enterprise in educational institutions; and
- To encourage the unemployed to create their own firms.

In addition to the above, the Development Research Centre signed an agreement for the implementation of the Women's Entrepreneurship and Leadership Development Project in Gaza. The Development Research Centre also held a two-week seminar to train instructors to form Palestinian entrepreneurs; this was funded by the Swedish International Development Agency.

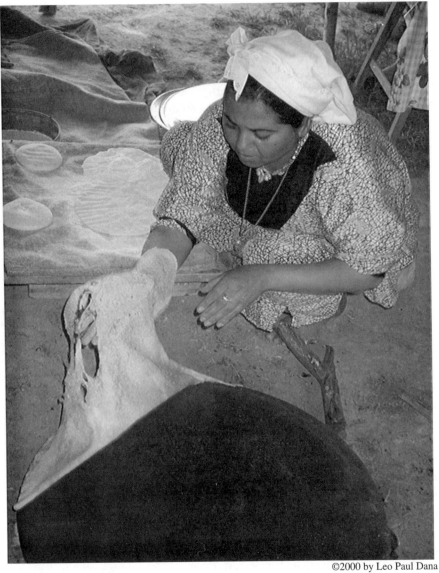

Making the Traditional Bread of Palestine

Toward the Future

Prior to the peace process, higher education was formally administered by the Israeli Civil Administration, and by the Palestinian High Education Counsel. In 1996, the Palestinian Authority established the Ministry of Higher Education, but the educational system continued to lack an enterprise component. If educational reform redesigns curricula with a focus on enterprise, then it is likely that more Palestinians will become increasingly interested in the business sector, and more importantly, the quality of management and entrepreneurship skills will likely improve.

Due to the anti-Israel boycott, production in Palestinian factories has been less than capacity – often two-thirds less than capacity. In the future, a normalisation of relations is bound to strengthen the Palestinian economy significantly.

©2000 by Leo Paul Dana

Diplomatic Representation in Laos

Chapter 12

The Syrian Arab Republic

Introduction

The Syrian Arab Republic, commonly known as Syria, shares land boundaries with Iraq, Israel, Jordan, Lebanon and Turkey. The country is approximately 185,000 square kilometres. Its capital, Damascus, is said to be the world's oldest continuously inhabited city. Aleppo, locally known as *Haleb*, has been a market centre since 2000 BC.

Historical Overview

Among the many peoples who have ruled Syria were the Semitic Amorites, the Hittites, the Assyrians, the Babylonians, the Persians, and the Aramaens who spread the Aramaic language throughout the region.

In 333 BC, Alexander the Great introduced Hellenic civilisation to the region. Following a period of rule by the Seleucids, Syria became a Roman province in 64 BC, and later a Byzantine province.

In 636 AD, Syria was conquered by Arab Muslims. It was later absorbed into the Islamic Empire of the Umayyad caliphs. Syria was known as *Biladul Sham* (Countries of Sham), at the time. Damascus was the capital of the Umayyad caliphate, until the 8th century.

The Crusaders arrived, from Europe, in 1096, and they integrated part of Syria into the Christian Kingdom of Jerusalem. They were defeated by Salah el Din. Following Mameluke rule, the Ottomans conquered Syria in 1516, and made it an Ottoman province.

Syria thrived under Ottoman rule. Venetian entrepreneurs, and other Europeans, established offices in Aleppo, an important market town and node along the desert trade routes between Persia and the West. However, the opening of the Suez Canal caused a decline in caravan trade, and Aleppo subsequently declined in economic importance. By the early 20th century, Damascus was linked to Beirut and to Medina by rail. Nevertheless, local entrepreneurs, including Jacob Safra, continued to prosper, by financing camel caravans. (Jacob's son Edmond later established the Republic National Bank of New York.)

During World War I, Britain promised the Syrians their independence, under the rule of Sherif Hussein Mecca of Saudi Arabia; Britain also pledged Syria as a French sphere of influence, as per the secret Sykes-Picot agreement between France and Great Britain. In 1919, the *Banque de Syrie* was established as a French company affiliate of the Ottoman Bank. Most of its shares were owned by French shareholders, and the balance by the Ottoman Bank. The *Banque de Syrie* issued the new Syrian currency, which was covered by French government bonds and by a French credit account, opened for the Levant, at the French Treasury. The Syrian pound could only be redeemed in Paris.

Victorious in the war, Emir Faisal was proclaimed king in 1920. He was the son of Hussein, Sherif of Mecca, and brother of King Abdullah of Iraq. However, no monarchy was established. Instead, the French exiled him. The League of Nations gave France a mandate over the Levant, and by decree from Paris, in 1920, the *Banque de Syrie* notes became the compulsory unit of contract in Syria. A series of treaties between 1920 and 1923 subdivided the territories taken from the Ottomans, formally creating and defining the Levant states, Lebanon and Syria.

When, in 1924, a convention was signed between the *Banque de Syrie* and the Levant states, the official bank of the Levant states was renamed the *Banque de Syrie et du Liban*. It was agreed that the currency issued by the bank would henceforth be redeemable in Marseilles, as well as in Paris. The currency remained pegged to the French franc until 1941, when it was linked to the Sterling.

Syria finally became independent in 1946. Syria joined Egypt to create the United Arab Republic, on February 1, 1958, and Syria was ruled, as a province, from Cairo, until the union was dissolved in 1961.

All large firms, in Syria, were nationalised during the 1960s. This included the banking and insurance sectors. Throughout this decade, national policy made the state a major player in the economy. The owner of a steam bath claimed that even his steam bath enterprise was nationalised in 1968. The private sector was largely agricultural.

Pistachios Grow in Abundance in Syria

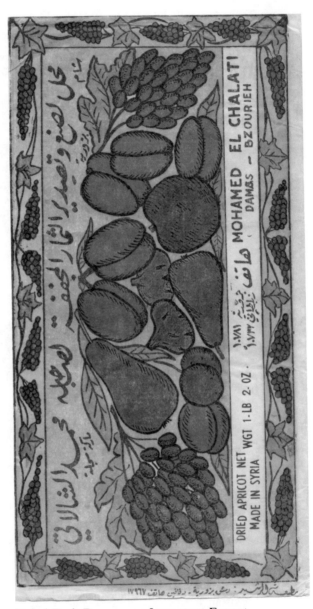

Dried Fruit Became an Important Export

Until the 1960s, industry in Syria was largely limited to textiles and food-processing. Important produce included almonds, apricots, barley, citrus fruit, cotton, figs, pistachios, pomegranates, sugar-beets and wheat.

© 2000 by Leo Paul Dana

Pomegranate Tree

During the 1970s, Syria's means to encourage industrialisation was an import-substitution model. Excluding agriculture, the public sector dominated the business sector, until the 1980s. Legislative Decree N°10 of 1986 accorded new privileges and benefits to new agricultural projects. In 1989, the oil and natural gas sector became a focus for investment.

By participating in the Gulf War of 1990, Syria gained access to substantial financial assistance. In 1991, private sector investment escalated, as liberalisation of the national economy encouraged foreign investment. During the early 1990s, the national economy grew by at least 7% per year, largely boosted by the agricultural and petroleum sectors.

Locally-grown Dates, Locally-grown Pomegranates, and Jordanian Guavas

Fresh Almonds

The mid-1990s saw record harvests, but declines in foreign investment and in oil production. Forty percent of the working population continued to work in agriculture, which accounted for about one third of GDP. Yet, the sector remained underdeveloped, with 80% of agricultural land dependent on rain. Fax machines were permitted in 1995, and satellite dishes in 1998. Scientific institutions were allowed access to the Internet in 1998, but the business sector was not.

According to the Labour Survey of 1998, 24.2% of the labour force (including 45.8% of women employees) were agricultural workers. At the time, 36.4% of the labour force consisted of production workers (see Table 12.1). Productivity varied by region; the average carpet-worker in Ain-al-Arab produced ten times as fast as that in Ahlaa. As indicated in Table 12.2, the number of self-employed persons was relatively high.

By 1999, industry (including food-processing) produced about one quarter of GDP. The state continued to control all strategic sectors of the economy, including banking, chemicals, electricity, oil, and much of the textile and food-processing industries.

Mobile phones were allowed into Syria, in 2000. Syrian President Hafez al-Assad died in June, that year. His son, Lieutenant-Colonel Bashar Assad then became Commander-in-Chief.

Economic prospects were brightened by talks for regional peace, which would improve the confidence of potential investors. Investment was required for agricultural and manufacturing projects, and to develop petroleum and gas production along the Euphrates River. However, defence continued to absorb about half of the national budget. Peace became more attractive than ever before.

Encouraging Private Enterprise

Many of the largest firms in Syria have been established by government decree and these operate outside the jurisdiction of the Syrian Commercial Law, contained in a legislative decree dating back to 1949. Nevertheless, there has been a shift away from a state-dominated economy. The Federation of the Syrian Chambers of Commerce is among the organisations assisting with the development of the private sector in Syria. Established in 1975, this federation represents fourteen chambers of commerce across the country. These include the Aleppo Chamber of Commerce and the Damascus Countryside Chamber of Commerce. The federation's Board of Directors includes the general directors of the Commercial Bank of Syria, the General Establishment for Trade & Distribution, and the General Company for Shoes. The federation supervises commercial, economic, and trade activities. It conducts research and hosts economic conferences. The Syrian National Committee for International Chambers of Commerce represents the joint economic interests of commerce, industry and infrastructure sectors, including banking and transport.

The Management Development & Productivity Centre also contributes to the private enterprise sector. It provides training in industrial engineering, and in personnel management. In addition, it prepares studies and provides advisory seminars.

The Scientific Studies & Research Centre focuses on applied technology and the promotion of selected industries, including electronics. Its aim is to link R & D with industry, and to transfer technologies to local industries. This centre has strong regional links, and a working relationship with the Arab School for Science & Technology. As well, it is affiliated with the Higher Institute for Applied Science & Technology, which conducts research in addition to providing training.

The Syrian European Business Centre, established by the European Union, promotes trade between Syrian enterprises and Europe. It is based in Damascus.

© 2000 by Leo Paul Dana

Heading Toward Latakia

Infrastructure

Syria enjoys two main ports along the Mediterranean Sea, namely Latakia and Tartus. Banyas is a port specialised in the export of oil. There are international airports at Damascus and Aleppo. The road network is good, and is supplemented by a rail system, used primarily to transport grains, phosphate and other commodities.

In July 1999, the Hijaz Railway established the Hijaz Express, involving four weekly links from Amman to Damascus, with an introductory fare equivalent to $3.50 for the seven-hour ride. The company overhauled three steam engines and three diesels for this service, estimating that the route would attract some 1,000 passengers a week. In December, frequency was reduced to three weekly trips, due to the lack of demand.

	MALE	FEMALE	TOTAL
Administration	9.3%	10.1%	9.4%
Agriculture	19.7%	45.8%	24.2%
Production	42.2%	8.4%	36.0%
Sales	12.6%	2.2%	10.8%
Service	6.2%	2.6%	5.6%
Technical & professional	10.0%	30.9%	13.6%
Total	100%	100%	100%

Table 12.1 Labour Force by Occupation

Source: 1998 Labour Force Survey, from the Ministry of Social Affairs &Labour

	MALE	FEMALE	TOTAL
Self-employed	29.5%	10.1%	26.2%
Employers	6.6%	0.6%	5.6%
Employees	56.3%	55.0%	56.1%
Unpaid Workers of Family Firms	7.6%	34.3%	12.1%
Total	100%	100%	100%

Table 12.2 Labour Distribution by Gender

Source: 1998 Labour Force Survey, from the Ministry of Social Affairs &Labour

The Workforce

Syria has an abundant and inexpensive workforce. Unemployment is in the 10% range. A high birth-rate contributes to the availability of labour. The minimum working age for children is 12 years old, and in some cases, a 9-hour day is permitted. This regulation applies only to paid employment, and not to family businesses. Children often participate in taking care of flocks belonging to their parents.

© 2000 by Leo Paul Dana

Well-tended Flock

In the formal, private enterprise sector, monthly minimum wage is $39 in rural regions and $42 in urban areas; this is according to figures provided in 2000, by the Ministry of Social Affairs & Labour, which is responsible for enforcing minimum wage. Temporary workers are not subject to minimum wage regulations.

Despite the abundance and low cost of labour, Syrian enterprises have had limited success in their haphazard attempt to penetrate international markets. With peace in the Middle East, Syrian entrepreneurs are likely to become successful sub-contractors to larger firms in high-cost producers. Syria could benefit from wealthy neighbours, as does Mexico from the United States, attracting capital investment and manufacturing for export.

The Golan Heights

Attracting Foreign Investment

Syria welcomes foreign direct investment, and allows non-Arabs to acquire real estate, provided a permit is granted. Free Zones have been established to facilitate the importation of goods for re-export.

Law N°10 of May 4, 1991 allows 100% foreign ownership of a firm, and provides accepted investors with certain privileges, provided that their projects involve at least 10 million Syrian pounds, and fall in certain sectors (including agriculture). Investors may then be exempted from the foreign exchange regulations imposed by Law N°24 of 1986. In addition, successful candidates are permitted to open a foreign currency account at the Commercial Bank of Syria. After five years, they may transfer out their net investment. Expatriate workers may export up to 50% of their earnings.

A foreign firm, which concludes more than one contract during any given year, is deemed to be a resident firm for taxation purposes; given that Syria has few double tax treaties, this can be problematic. A solution is to create a company in Cyprus, and to let this entity conduct business in Syria; Cyprus is among the very few nations to have a tax agreement with Syria.

© 2000 by Leo Paul Dana

Foreign Investment Bringing a Taste of the West

Toward the Future

The state of war has been costly for Syria. Enterprises were made to pay a War Effort Tax surcharge, equal to 30% of income tax payable. In Damascus, the Special Bureau for Boycotting Israel limited trade with Syria's southern neighbour.

Peace will allow more money to be redirected to the benefit of the Syrian people. The *Jordan Times,* cover-story on December 7 (1999), reported a demand, in Syria, for Israeli technology. The open exchange of goods, services and technology, in a scenario of comprehensive regional peace can contribute to the mutual benefit of all.

The abundance of inexpensive labour, coupled with fertile land and the abundance of oil, gas and phosphate, suggest a bright potential for Syria. It appears that regional peace will lead to rapid development. Sectors expected to see exceptional growth include the processing of agricultural products and the manufacturing of textiles and clothing. The demand for fertiliser should increase as agriculture is developed.

Chapter 13

The Republic of Turkey

Introduction

Turkey covers 780,580 square kilometres, stretching from Europe to Asia, and neighbouring Armenia, Bulgaria, Georgia, Greece, Iran, Iraq and Syria. It has traditionally served as a cross-roads of trade, and a hub of the Silk Road. At various times in history, entrepreneurs from central Asia brought ideas, innovations, technologies and trade from the east, to the area known, in modern times, as Turkey. This land became central to the Silk Road, linking Europe with Asia. Chinese silk would transit through here, before being sold in ancient Rome. From the Roman Empire, entrepreneurs passed by, transporting coins, coral, glass, pottery and textiles bound for China.

Two millennia later, Istanbul is still home to the archetype of the structured bazaar, and entrepreneurs are still central to society. Loyalty to the extended family serves as a springboard to launch new enterprises. The small business sector is gaining importance, and in recent years, Turkish entrepreneurs have been bringing development to the formerly Soviet republics of central Asia. These include Kazakhstan, the Kyrgyz Republic, Tajikistan, Turkmenistan, and Uzbekistan. Dana (1997a; 1997b) discusses entrepreneurship in Kazakhstan, while the Kyrgyz Republic is the topic of Dana (2000a).

Turkey's economy is something of a miracle.
— The Economist, June 8, 1996, p.8.

Historical Overview

The Anatolian Plateau, which covers the bulk of today's Republic of Turkey, was settled approximately 6000 BC, at which time people from the east established primitive farming communities. About 1800 BC, the area was invaded by people from central Asia, who had already made use of iron. Then came Greeks and other Indo-Europeans, and it was here that during the 7th century BC, the Lydians produced the earliest coins known to us today. About 546 BC, the settlements came under Persian rule, until Persia was overthrown by Alexander the Great two centuries later.

In the year 67 BC, the region was absorbed by the Romans. When the Roman Empire was divided during the 3rd century, a Greek city, Byzantium, became the capital of the eastern sector, which came to be known as the Byzantine Empire. In the year 328, the Christian emperor Constantine moved here from Rome, and Byzantium's name was changed to Constantinople.

In 1403, an ambassador from Spain came to Constantinople, the Byzantine capital at the time. In his diary, he remarked that he was greatly impressed by the great number of warehouses, and the tremendous mercantile activity, with cargo carried on the backs of porters.

For centuries the inter-continental Byzantine Empire flourished, but a Turkic-speaking tribe, the Ottomans, gradually occupied it. The last Byzantine emperor, Constantine XI, was killed in battle and the Ottomans ultimately captured Constantinople in 1453, under the leadership of Sultan Mohammed (Mehmet) II. Suddenly, this city became the heart of the Ottoman Empire. In addition to having political power, the Ottoman sultan was also caliph of Islam.

The Ottoman Empire reached its zenith under Suleiman the Magnificent, who ruled from 1520 to 1566. At the time, the Ottoman Empire extended as far west as Hungary and Transylvania; the empire stretched into the Balkan Peninsula, including Greece, and from Asia Minor to Azerbaijan, Mesopotamia, the Arabian peninsula, and into North Africa. The Ottomans dominated Egypt and Sudan, and penetrated Ethiopia as well as Libya.

Authority in the Ottoman Empire was highly decentralised. Non-Muslim ethnic groups each had its own religious leader, who reported to the sultan. The principal ethnic communities were the Armenians, the Greek Orthodox, and the Jews – all of whom had considerable autonomy. Greek and Jewish merchants conducted important trade with the West, providing substantial revenue to the empire.

At the beginning of the 17th century, when tobacco was being introduced to the Orient, the doctors of Islamic law declared the use of tobacco as impure. During the reign of Sultan Mourat IV, who ruled from 1623 to 1640, smoking tobacco was punishable by death.

In 1826, England and Russia helped Greece achieve independence from the Ottomans. Soon after, Algeria and Tunis were lost to France and Tripoli to Italy, while England took control of Egypt.

During World War I, the Ottoman Empire joined the central powers, and, in 1915, the Allied forces were defeated at Gallipoli. Nevertheless, the British were very successful in the Middle East. They crossed the Sinai, penetrated Palestine and set off to capture Jerusalem.

© 2000 by Leo Paul Dana

Memorial to New Zealanders Who Fell in Palestine, Egypt & Gallipoli

Commanded by General Sir Edmund Allenby and assisted by the Arab followers of Colonel T. E. Lawrence – Lawrence of Arabia – the British occupied Jerusalem and pushed the Ottomans out of greater Palestine and Syria further north.   While Syria was given to France, Palestine became British, and most of it eventually became the Hashemite Kingdom of Jordan.

In 1920, the last sultan accepted defeat.   The Turkish War of Independence lasted until 1922. The following year, in July 1923, the Treaty of Lausanne recognised the independence of the Republic of Turkey. Army commander Mustafa Kemal became its first president, and changed his name to Kemal Atatürk, literally father of the Turks. The national capital was moved from Constantinople to Ankara; the name of Constantinople was changed to Istanbul.

The new country allowed ethnic Turks, residing in British Cyprus, to opt for British citizenship. In 1925, Turkey opened a consulate in Larnaca, to assist people in obtaining Turkish documents. About 10,000 Cypriots obtained Turkish nationality, although slightly over half moved to Turkey.

Atatürk decided to westernise Turkey. He forced his subjects to adopt surnames and he banned the fez – known in Arabic as *tarboush* – a cone-shaped head-cover traditional to the Ottomans. In 1928, the Latin alphabet replaced Arabic script in Turkey, and Turks began to read from left to right. In 1930, women in Turkey were given the right to vote. In 1945, a land reform bill distributed large tracts of agricultural land to peasants who had none.

The Turkish currency tumbled during the late 20th century, from a rate of 14 liras to the dollar in 1970, to 164 liras per dollar in 1982, 872 liras per dollar in 1987, 2,608 liras per dollar in 1990, 6,896 liras per dollar in 1992, 82,000 liras per dollar in 1996, 190,500 liras per dollar in 1997, 286,275 liras per dollar in 1998, and 480,975 liras per dollar in 1999.

Istanbul & the Bazaar Economy

Known as Byzantium, later as Constantinople and ultimately as Istanbul, this city has been a centre of international entrepreneurship for 2,000 years. The city was, at various times, desired by the Greeks, the Persians, the Macedonians, the Romans, the Crusaders and the Ottomans. Spanning the Bosphorus Strait, Istanbul is the only city in the world built on two continents.

One Million Lira Note

The Bosphorus Strait connects the Black Sea with the Sea of Marmara, separating Europe from Asia. According to the Montreux Convention, this sea route must be kept open to all merchant vessels.

Like Jerusalem, Pittsburgh and Rome, Istanbul is built on seven hills. Istanbul is the former capital of three successive empires: the Roman, Byzantine and Ottoman Empires. For sixteen centuries, this eclectic city dominated Asia Minor, and traders from three continents came here to trade with entrepreneurs who controlled international trade. Although it has long lost its status as imperial capital, Istanbul is still the most important trading centre in Turkey.

Istanbul's central market is the Kapali Carsi, literally meaning "the covered market." It was developed under Mehmet II, the Ottoman sultan who captured the city in 1453. Eventually, this complex came to cover a surface area of 32 hectares. It has 18 separate gates. Also referred to as the Grand Bazaar, this highly organised market is known around the world as the archetype of the structured bazaar.

At various times, bows and arrows, turbans, hashish and opium were sold in this market. Until slavery was abolished in 1847, it was also possible to purchase slaves here. After the great fire of 1954, this market was greatly renovated, giving it a much-modernised appearance. The benches were removed, while stalls were refurbished with panels of aluminium and glass. Further modifications were made during the 1980s.

Kapali Carsi

Every day, half a million people walk by here. This bazaar is the workplace of some 2,000 people dealing in gold, and each year, approximately 100 tons of gold exchange hands here. Much gold will be smuggled.

Another of Istanbul's bazaars is the Egyptian Market, built during the mid-1600s, by Hatik the Empress, mother of the future sultan, Mehmet IV. This market was built on the site of a Venetian trading counter, on the shores of the Golden Horn. Herbs, spices and dried fruit are sold here. In former times, much of the merchandise came from Cairo; this is how the Egyptian Market got its name.

There are also several fish markets in Istanbul. Upon entering any of the many bazaars, one encounters a multitude of scents.

©2000 by Leo Paul Dana

The Bazaar Economy in Kilis, Near the Syrian Border

New venture creation has long been perceived as important in this society. Records indicate that during the 17th century, there were 1,100 professional guilds in Istanbul alone. Although the guilds of the bazaar economy never had a power equivalent to those of western Europe, fees were nevertheless collected from members, and funds were accumulated. Some of this money was used to grant loans to new enterprises. Although each of these associations had an elected president, hierarchy within the organisations of the bazaar was less structured than in Occidental counterparts.

An apprentice in western Europe was dependent on his master and subordinate to him – he was therefore expected to be submissive to the master. In contrast, the greatest difference between a master and an apprentice, in Turkey, is simply professional qualification.

A problem, in the bazaar, is that undeclared transactions make tax-collection difficult. Yet, typical of the bazaar economy, not everybody at a market has an economic motive. Some come to buy and others are here to sell, yet others have their own motivations, such as socialising.

The Firm-Type Economy

While the complex bazaar economy thrives to this day, a firm-type economy has also taken root in Turkey. A state-dominated firm-type economy emerged prior to World War II, and family-owned business groups began to flourish during the 1950s.

Today, the big business sector in Turkey is dominated by family-controlled and diversified groups, somewhat comparable to the *chaebols* of Korea; this is elaborated upon by Bugra (1994). Also central to the Turkish economy are thousands of family businesses, providing jobs for the extended family. In particular, the government has recognised the importance of a healthy small business sector within it. With this in mind, a government body known as the Small and Medium Industry Development Organisation (KOSGEB) was established, to assist entrepreneurs in the formal firm-type economy. KOSGEB operates as a non-profit, semi-autonomous organisation. Board members include government representatives and people from the private sector. The mission of KOSGEB is four-fold: (i) to develop and support the mechanisms, which would increase the competitive capacity of small and medium-scale industries, in domestic and international markets; (ii) to disseminate appropriate information to small and medium-scale industries; (iii) to provide new job opportunities in market and technology-oriented high value added production fields; and (iv) to encourage entrepreneurship and to realise the above-mentioned activities in accordance with programme targets and planned priorities.

The primary objective of KOSGEB is to improve the efficiency and competitive capacity of small and medium-scale industries in Turkey. This includes developing technological skills, improving managerial infrastructure, and resolving financial, technical and marketing problems. KOSGEB in Turkey functions in a way similar to that of the Small Business Administration in the United States. Its two-fold service policy is: to provide qualified and rapid services to small and medium-scale industries, in order to help them improve quality standards, while maintaining competitive prices; and to eliminate all the obstacles that might confront small and medium-scale industries. KOSGEB operates three institutes: the Regional Development Institute; the Entrepreneurship Development Institute; and the Market Research and Export Promotion Institute. It also operates 27 Small Business Development Centres, seven Technology Development Centres, and a Consultancy Centre.

Firm-Type Economy

KOSGEB offers specialised programmes on: organisational infrastructure improvement; quality development and total quality systems; technological activities development and support; financial support mechanisms development; exporting and marketing activities development; regional/local industries development; new job opportunities and entrepreneurship support; and information systems and electronic commerce.

While such programmes are generally successful in training entrepreneurs, in updating technology, and in day-to-day management issues such as quality control, other difficulties remain. To this end, non-governmental organisations may be helpful.

A non-governmental organisation was established in 1990, for the purpose of promoting the interests of entrepreneurs. Officially called *Türkiye Orta Ölçekli Isletmeler Serbest Meslek Mensuplari ve Yöneticiler Vakfi*, it is known by the acronym TOSYÖV. In English, this translates to the Turkish Foundation for Small and Medium Enterprises.

The foundation defined a small or medium-scaled business as having 5 to 200 employees; both private and public firms fitting this description may be members. The goals of TOSYÖV, include:

- To organise promotion and efficient representation of small and medium-scaled enterprises in Turkey;
- To develop special training, further education and consulting for Turkish entrepreneurs;
- To create a financially sound infrastructure for small and medium enterprises, including a fair subsidy-system, sufficient financial resources and adequate possibilities for investment;
- To obtain new technologies for Turkish enterprises, in order to achieve higher quality, more competitive products, and more efficiently;
- To develop a databank for small and medium-sized firms in Turkey;
- To build good public relations;
- To press for reforms ensuring a reduction in tax burden; and
- To strengthen the international contacts of small and medium-sized businesses in Turkey.

The organisation provides the following services through its several branches in different provinces of Turkey:

- Project and consulting services in each needed area such as domestic and foreign trade, marketing, finance, production;
- Long-term credit programmes with low interest rates;
- Short and long-term policies and a rational competition in a balanced structured market;
- Incentive starter programmes for young entrepreneurs;
- Training seminars on marketing, feasibility studies, etc.
- PROFIL, the TOSYÖV consulting company, which supports non-members as well as non-members;
- A Credit Guarantee Fund which has been established both to help the entrepreneurs on guarantees and to reduce excessive bank bureaucracies;
- Lobby for small and medium-sized enterprises in the Turkish Parliament;
- Insurance service;
- A regular TOSYÖV letter and a general publication programme to voice the problems of Turkish small and medium business; and

- Co-operation with other organisations, including the Konrad Adenauer Foundation, the Turkish government, the Union of Chambers of Industry and Commerce (TOBB), the Confederation of Turkish Small Scale Industry and Handicrafts (TSEK), and the Foundation for Promotion of Vocational Training and Small Industry (MEKSA), as well as KOSGEB.

Public Policy

Prior to the creation of modern Turkey, most business in the Ottoman Empire was conducted by Greeks, Jews, and Armenians. The Turks tended to work on farms or join the military or public service.

After independence, a policy of protectionism prevailed. Much industry was state-owned, and required protection. High tariffs and import bans remained in place until the 1970s.

Apertura changed the environment for business. During the 1980s, the government embarked on an export promotion programme. Exporters were offered rebates on energy and transportation. In addition, 30% of export costs were paid by the state. These subsidies were later repealed, to comply with European Union regulations.

During the 1990s, 60% of the financial sector and 50% of manufacturing was still owned by the government. Public policy mobilised state funds to encourage small and medium firms, in the private sector. The state provided grants to small-scale exporters.

Toward the Future

From a geographical perspective, Turkey has historically been an important cross-road of intercontinental trade, and a central hub of the Silk Road (see also Dana, 2000c.)

In modern times, a firm-type economy has emerged in Turkey, alongside the traditional bazaar economy. Both governmental and non-governmental efforts have contributed to today's growing business sector in Turkey. While cotton is Turkey's major export crop, the nation is the world's largest producer of hazelnuts and sultana raisins. Turkey is also Europe's principal exporter of textiles.

The Ascensor in Izmir, Meeting Place of Entrepreneurs

Pan-Turkic trade between Turkey and newly-independent republics of the CIS is on the rise. In 1992, Turkey forged links with CIS countries. That same year, Turkey joined a co-operative economic scheme for countries bordering the Black Sea. By the mid-1990s, Russia was Turkey's second largest trading partner. In 1996, Turkey entered a customs union with the European Union. In April, that year, Turkey also announced the details of a defence pact with Israel. At the dawn of the 21st century, Turkey is facing a bright future.

© 2000 by Leo Paul Dana

The Blue Mosque

Chapter 14

The Turkish Republic of Northern Cyprus

Introduction

In contrast to the Republic of Cyprus – which covers the southern part of the same island – the Turkish Republic of Northern Cyprus (TRNC) is a newer political entity, which most countries have never recognised. The TRNC has long been the object of an international economic boycott. The nature of enterprise here – isolated from the world economy – is very reflective of local culture and related values.

People in the TRNC consider it to be a religious entity. Its flag consists of an Islamic crescent and star between two stripes.

©2000 by Leo Paul Dana

Reading Qur-an

Historical Overview

There have been Turks in Cyprus since the Ottoman invasion of 1571, at which time they brought Islam to the island. In 1572, 1,689 families moved from Anatolia to Cyprus. A decentralised Ottoman administration – based on communal self-rule – lasted until 1878, when the administration of Cyprus was handed to England, although the island remained legally Ottoman territory.

Early Ottoman Postage Stamp

In 1914, England declared the annexation of Cyprus to Great Britain; the Turkish government accepted this annexation with the Treaty of Sevres, in 1920. Nevertheless, even when Cyprus became a British colony, in 1925, Turkish Cypriots continued to live here.

© 2000 by Leo Paul Dana

Remnants of British Rule in Northern Cyprus

By World War II, ethnic consciousness became apparent. In 1944, the publisher of a Turkish-language daily in Cyprus established the Cyprus Turkish National People's Party. In 1950, the Bishop of Kition was elected as Archbishop Makarious III; he pledged to strive for the unification of Cyprus with Greece.

On 16 August 1960, the island became a republic, with Makarious its first president. As had been the case in the Indian sub-continent, a generation earlier, independence led to increased strife between ethnic groups in Cyprus. Clashes between Christian Greeks and Muslim Turks, on the island, led to the segregation of the two groups in 1963.

By 1964, one in four Turkish Cypriots was displaced. Makarious imposed an embargo on Turkish enclaves in Cyprus, banning fuel, cement, shoelaces and Red Cross supplies.

In June 1974, Turkish troops landed on the northern coast of Cyprus – on the premise that their motive was to protect the interest of their fellow Muslims on the island – and took control of 37% of the nation's area. While Turkish Cypriots saw this as liberation from Christian domination, the Greek Cypriots termed this an illegal occupation. In any event, the result was the declaration of the Turkish Federated State of Kibris, on February 13, 1975.

Separating the two entities of Cyprus is the Green Line – a United Nations buffer zone – 180 kilometres long and covering 4% of the island's land surface. Until the creation of this boundary, both sides of Cyprus shared a common history, one government, a unified infrastructure, and equal access to foreign markets. Then, significant changes were introduced.

The Turks expelled 180,000 Christians from the Turkish Federated State of Kibris, and brought Turkish-speaking Muslim immigrants from Turkey. Whereas English, Greek and Turkish had been common prior to the split, the Turkish authorities in Cyprus opted for one official national language – Turkish. Monolingual, Turkish signs replaced bilingual and trilingual signs. The new government also changed the names of towns, replacing Greek names by Turkish ones.

On November 15, 1983, the president of the Turkish Federated State of Kibris declared the independence of the TRNC. With the exception of Turkey, however, no country would recognise this new, self-declared nation.

The Border at Nicosia/Lefkoşa

The Turkish Republic of Northern Cyprus

Upon first glance, much of Cyprus carries the same physical traits as do neighbouring Greek and Turkish islands. Terrace farming is common along the slopes of the TRNC. During their invasion, however, the Turks bombed much of the lush forests on the island.

The fortified Green Line cuts through the capital city, just as the Berlin Wall once divided Berlin. Turkish and Turkish Cypriot troops watch the Greek Cypriot National Guardsmen, across a narrow, weed-covered street. Soldiers patrol the streets and are sometimes the only people in sight.

Ninety-eight percent of the people in the TRNC are Muslim. They are often more concerned with isolation from Christian values, than with economic issues. They have no qualms about expressing their feelings of hatred for Greeks and Christians alike. Opinions are offered most openly. Billboards illustrate pictures of the war in which Orthodox priests were said to have killed Muslims. Postcards carry prose describing the Muslims as innocent victims.

© 2000 by Leo Paul Dana

After the War

A quarter of a century after the cease-fire it still feels like the war has just ended; bullet holes mark many walls and monuments. One church has become a mosque. Another is now a store. Partially-standing ruins of the war can be seen everywhere. These are grim reminders of the mass shootings and looting of the past. Antique shops display many beautiful pieces that one cannot help but to imagine have been stolen from former residents who were moved from their homes. The irony lies in the fact that, should tourists make a purchase, such pieces will be confiscated upon departure from the TRNC as these are not legally exportable.

© 2000 by Leo Paul Dana

Former Church Converted to Mosque with Minaret

In protest of the TRNC and of its actions, the international community has enforced an embargo on this entity. Officially, no country other than Turkey has trade links or transportation links with the TRNC. Thus, in contrast to the Republic of Cyprus, which is industrialised and export-oriented, the TRNC is largely shut off from the global economy. Few respondents, interviewed by the author, attribute economic problems to the international boycott; however, the overwhelming majority of interviewees in the TRNC suggest that the boycott is not a major problem when compared to the "threat" of Americanisation. Turkish Cypriots claim that isolation from Christianity and from Western values is spiritually more important for them than is any material impact of the embargo. Furthermore, most are happy that Turkish has replaced the English language in the TRNC; they are more open to Arabic as a second language than to a language from the West.

The Economy

In contrast to the outward-looking economy of the Republic of Cyprus, that of the TRNC is limited by the fact that the latter is not recognised by any international organisation. As a result of the economic embargo, the TRNC has no official economic ties with any country outside Turkey. Government sources suggest that the TRNC workforce consists of 74,000 people and 25% are employed in agriculture.

© 2000 by Leo Paul Dana

Sheep Grazing Among Olive Trees

Agriculture is the backbone of the TRNC economy. While agriculture in the Republic of Cyprus is export-oriented, that in the TRNC is usually limited to subsistence activity. Cereals, citrus fruits, grapes and olives are grown for local consumption. Sheep and goats are bred. Farmers sometimes own cattle, horses and mules as well. Farming methods are unsophisticated and food production is less than is demand; although most of the TRNC is agricultural land, food – including cereals and olives – must be imported from Turkey.

© 2000 by Leo Paul Dana

The Economy is Highly Dependent on That of Turkey

TRNC exports, such as carton and cookware, receive special treatment in Turkey. However, the overwhelming growth of industries in Turkey during the mid-1990s, along with the lowering of Turkey's import tariffs, has resulted in the erosion of the market share of TRNC products.

Other than the production of cardboard boxes and of clothing, manufacturing in the TRNC is largely limited to the processing of agricultural produce. Citrus juice is made into concentrate and peels are turned into animal fodder.

The TRNC has no comparative advantage in industry; Turkey is actually quite strong in the produce-processing and textile industries. Consequently, most of the industrial production in the TRNC must be absorbed by limited local demand. Furthermore, to the detriment of small-scale manufacturers in the TRNC, low tariffs on Turkish imports into the TRNC are allowing Turkish goods to flood the local market.

Manufacturing's relative share of fixed investment in the TRNC has been declining due to the inability to attract new investment or to establish new industries. Meanwhile, increased efficiency among manufacturers in Turkey is limiting the TRNC's potential in the latter's only export market.

Another problem in the TRNC is derived from the fact that due to high rates of inflation, basic wages are subject to indexing. A commission – comprised of employers, government representatives and trade officials from among fifteen unions – adjusts wages. Its representation is a source of contention as the union movement claims that the government is siding heavily with employers. This may be explained by the fact that the government is itself a major employer.

While entrepreneurship is the major source of employment in the Republic of Cyprus, the TRNC government has been creating often-redundant jobs for the purpose of reducing unemployment figures. Hence, the official unemployment rate ignores substantial under-employment.

An employer must pay social security contributions for his employees. This is between 10 and 15.5% of earnings. In addition, a minimum of 5% is paid to the Provident Fund.

Per capita, GNP in the TRNC is one quarter that in the Republic of Cyprus. Real growth in the TRNC has been negative, and inflation has surpassed an annual rate of 200%.

Interviewees reported to the author that the fastest growing sector has been heroin traffic. The Turkish government sends financial aid to its puppet republic – about 35% of the TRNC's GDP.

Infrastructure and Public Policy

The TRNC inherited a well-developed infrastructure. Funds from Saudi Arabia contributed to the upgrading of the road between Girne (formerly Kyrenia) and Lefkoşa (as Nicosia is referred to locally).

Travel within the TRNC is not problematic. However, international transportation links have been almost completely severed, including passage to the opposite side of the same island. Anyone, who has entered the TRNC from Gazi Magusa (formerly Famagusta) or Girne, would be arrested if attempting to cross to the Republic of Cyprus.

Road-sign at Round-about

Other than to and from mainland Turkey, the TRNC has no international links whatsoever. No airport or harbour in the TRNC is recognised by the international community and all are considered illegal. The flag-carrier of the TRNC is Cyprus Turkish Airlines, but it only flies between Turkey and the Encan International Airport at Tymbou in the TRNC.

Until late 1997, there were only three telephone lines linking the TRNC with the Republic of Cyprus. The United Nations controlled the lines and calls were connected manually by an operator. Connections were made only between 7 a.m. and 10 p.m. In November 1997 Turkish Cypriot entrepreneurs met with Greek Cypriots at a conference in Brussels where both sides expressed interest in improved telecommunication facilities between the two sides. There, they agreed to expand telephone services at a cost of $150,000 – to include 20 automatic lines, useable 24 hours a day. The United States paid for the system.

The banking infrastructure in the TRNC is still very limited. In May 1983, the Cyprus pound was banned here, and it became subject to foreign exchange regulations. Since the Turkish lira has become the sole medium of exchange in the TRNC, monetary policy and exchange rates have been a function of decisions made in Istanbul. The central bank of the TRNC, therefore, has a limited scope of activity. Since the collapse of the Everest Bank and the Mediterranean Guarantee Bank, both in 1994, the principal financial institutions in the TRNC have been Islamic banks and Islamic investment companies. Commercial lending rates are 30% above the inflation rate.

Accounts may only be opened in Turkish lira, the value of which has been dropping rapidly. In 1987, $1 US bought 872 Turkish liras; in 1990, $1 US bought 2,608 liras. In 1996 $1 was worth 82,000 liras and by 1999 $1 bought 480,975 liras.

© 2000 by Leo Paul Dana
The Faisal Islamic Bank of Kibris Ltd.

In accordance with Exchange Control legislation, no foreign investor may engage in business in the TRNC unless special approval has been obtained from the Ministry of Finance in Lefkoşa. Many Turkish Cypriots have left the island and become entrepreneurs in London. These are the subject of Ladbury (1984).

Procedures for Foreign Investment in the TRNC

Foreigners, whether individuals or corporate bodies, must respect considerable paperwork requirements before conducting business in the TRNC. Forms are supplied from the Department of the Official Receiver and Registrar – when they are available.

The first step along the application procedure is to supply a Special Project Feasibility Form, filled in quadruplicate. An additional application must be filled with the Official Receiver and Registrar.

A foreigner wishing to become a shareholder in the TRNC must subscribe a minimum of $30,000. Yet, foreign investors are allowed only a minority holding, unless special permission is obtained from the Council of Ministers. Persons from outside Turkey must pay in foreign currency.

Entrepreneurs from overseas and wishing to launch new ventures must supply a sum of at least $30,000, excluding fixed capital assets. The Ministry of Economy and Finance may raise this amount, at its discretion. In addition, a business permit must be obtained from the local Migration Office.

Companies already established overseas need permission from the Council of Ministers, in order to operate in the TRNC; the applicant must also transfer to the TRNC an amount of not less than $30,000 in convertible foreign currency, or the Turkish lira equivalent in the case of a Turkish firm. In addition, individuals coming from abroad require a permit from the Department of Immigration, in order to participate in the administration of a corporate entity. Prior to purchasing immovable property in the TRNC, permission is required from the Ministry of the Interior.

To engage in importing, a firm must register with the Chamber of Commerce or the Chamber of Industry. Also, a permit is required, from the Department of Trade.

Trademarks already registered abroad may be considered for registration in the TRNC. If accepted, a trade-mark may be registered for seven years, with a possibility of renewal thereafter.

Tourism

No country, other than Turkey, permits traffic to or from the TRNC either by air or sea. On a ferry from mainland Turkey, overstuffed baggage is piled over a metre high, on hand-made trolleys. Passengers wearing soiled clothes line the corridors and main decks, while their numerous children are left to roam. Many are Anatolian Turks coming to settle in formerly Greek villages, the inhabitants of which are gone.

Once the vessel has docked at Gazi Magusa, a port considered illegal by international authorities, immigration rituals begin. The disorderly line-ups behind the barred gates add to the increasing pressure on people's nerves.

It is not uncommon for a physical fight to break out in front of the customs control desk and perhaps another one behind the gate. It will be hours before all pass through. Some will have their passports stamped, while many will choose not to, because a TRNC stamp in a passport bars the bearer from entering Greece.

Signs in Gazi Magusa indicate where hotels and where tourist facilities once existed; many establishments have been boarded up. The newspaper *Kibris Northern Cyprus Monthly* quoted England's *Financial Times* of July 26, 1997, explaining that "because visitors have to travel there via Turkey, few bother (*Kibris Northern Cyprus Monthly*, 1997, p. 6)." In fact the TRNC receives only 30,000 visitors a year; the small Venetian port, Girne, is popular – mostly among English and German visitors.

People in the TRNC are concerned about tourism due to the Western values it brings. "Some tourists wish to eat sinful food, such as bacon." Another interviewee explained, "Exposure to foreigners can threaten our future, by misleading our youth into thinking bellybutton rings and tongue rings are acceptable."

Recreational Vessel

Toward the Future

Entrepreneurs from both sides of Cyprus have improved trans-border communications and are forging co-operation between their respective nations. Each Monday, Turkish Cypriot entrepreneurs from the TRNC meet prominent Greek Cypriot entrepreneurs from the Republic of Cyprus; they get together at the Fulbright Centre, in the United Nations buffer zone. Here, they discuss the entrepreneurial activities that they might engage in, as soon as their governments allow them to.

Meanwhile, business is limited by the man-made Green Line – a line of hatred. As discussed by Dana and Dana (2000), the means to a prosperous enterprise sector throughout this island appears to be tolerance by both sides and of both sides – their peoples, their cultures, their religions and their values.

Typical Couple in Northern Cyprus

Chapter 15

Toward the Future

Not long ago, industrial development, along the Eastern Mediterranean, was quite limited. More recently, governments have successfully improved the infrastructure of their countries, and they have created incentives for business investors. Even Albania, which had a backward economy until the early 1990s, is forging ahead and is being praised for its economic achievements.

This book has introduced, to the reader, the different economies of the Eastern Mediterranean. Striking contrasts exist, even between neighbours. While most firms registered in the Republic of Cyprus are offshore companies, the typical entrepreneur in the TRNC is a subsistence farmer. While life in the Republic of Cyprus is often focused on material gain, life in the TRNC revolves around religion and cultural identity; Islamic banks and Islamic investment companies are central to the economy. Indeed the economic development of a nation cannot but reflect the values and priorities of its ethnic composition. By the same token, we note that the man-made Green Line has limited business in Cyprus. Yet entrepreneurs, from both sides of Cyprus, are forging co-operation. By being tolerant of one another – different religions, cultures, and values – both sides stand to gain.

What countries of the Eastern Mediterranean have in common, is that they have been changing very quickly, and their economies are set for rapid growth, especially during times of peace. Since Egypt recognised the need to create 450,000 new jobs annually, the target has been to increase exports by 11% annually. The recent agreement to increase trade between Egypt and Turkey is among several policy measures to facilitate international trade. Trade between Egypt and Israel (Egypt's second biggest trading partner in the region of the Middle East and North Africa), includes 2 million tons of crude oil, in addition to non-oil trade amounting to almost $100 million. If half a million Israeli tourists would visit Egypt each year, this would add another $750 million to the Egyptian economy.

Producing for Export

© 2000 by Leo Paul Dana

Quality Control

© 2000 by Leo Paul Dana

Packaging Pharmaceuticals for Export

© 2000 by Leo Paul Dana

Harnessing Technology

Greece has been exporting technology to its neighbours with emerging economies. Since the end of the wars in Yugoslavia, Greek enterprises have been at the forefront of economic development in the Balkans; while Greek banks have been financing progress, Greek entrepreneurs have been innovating and providing a variety of services in the region.

With the largest number of high-tech start-ups (in absolute terms) after the United States, Israel has become nicknamed the new Silicon Valley. Local firms have excelled in agro-technology, biotechnology, computer-assisted education, data-communication, electronics, encryption, and software development. A recent Israeli invention uses solar technology to generate electricity using solar-heated air to operate a turbine.

Peace between Israel and Jordan has led to the creation of QIZs in Jordan. These provide joint projects between Israelis, Jordanian and Palestinians with preferential treatment into the United States.

The end of the civil war in Lebanon has likewise improved the economy. Investment is being attracted to the low income tax schedule and the liberal economic policy in force in Lebanon. The nation is once again becoming a banking centre, popularly known as the Switzerland of the Middle East.

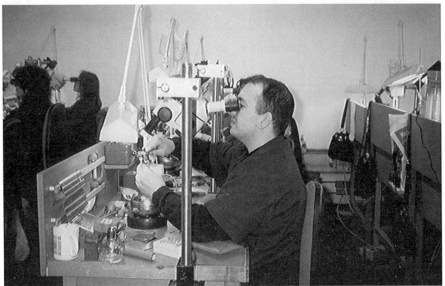

Looking into the Future

Peace will also bring prosperity to the Palestinians. While the QIZs have given a boost to manufacturing, the new airport at Gaza is contributing to an improved infrastructure.

Syria too is facing a new era, especially since Bashar Assad took over from his father, during the second quarter of 2000.

Turkish enterprises, meanwhile, are prospering while contributing to the development of the Turkic republics of central Asia.

Proctor (2000) reported an interview with Arkia, a Tel Aviv-based airline, which is part of a group that has acquired 75% stake in Balkan Bulgarian Airlines. Having recently participated in the launching of a new airline in Nigeria, Arkia was already planning the expansion of its own route network, to destinations it expected to open up, with advances toward regional peace. The airline's route to Sharm el Sheikh is written into the Camp David peace accord, and airline executives expect that a broader peace will boost regional tourism. Mr. Israel Borovich, President and Chief Executive Officer of Arkia was quoted as saying, "Peace will prevail. It's not a process anyone can stop."

Toward the Future

For several decades, the lack of a comprehensive peace in the Middle East has stunted growth in the region, and military expenditures kept back economic development. With peace in the air, the countries of the Eastern Mediterranean will be in a better position to capitalise on the potential of their region.

The Eastern Mediterranean is blessed with mineral resources, and oil is being supplemented by solar energy, which is being harnessed to produce power. In addition, skilled labour is plentiful and inexpensive in this part of the world; emphasis on training and research has been furthering knowledge and improving skills. The use of technology is spreading rapidly. A rising middle class is providing an excellent local market. All this, coupled with recent economic reforms has been attracting unprecedented investment.

Technology, energy, and access to affordable wages all contribute to economic power. The Eastern Mediterranean has all these factors in abundance.

The wars of the 20th century restrained economic progress in the region. Peace, in contrast, will allow this region to play an increasingly prominent role in the world economy, in the very near future. The potential of the Eastern Mediterranean should not be ignored.

Bibliography

Barth, Frederik (1963), *The Role of the Entrepreneur and Social Change in Northern Norway,* Bergen, Norway: Norwegian Universities Press.

Barth, Frederik (1967), "On the Study of Social Change," *American Anthropologist* 69 (6), pp. 661-669.

Brockhaus, Robert H., Sr. (1991), "Entrepreneurship, Education and Research Outside North America," *Entrepreneurship, Theory & Practice* 15 (3), Spring, pp. 77-84.

Bugra, Ayse (1994), *State and Business in Modern Turkey,* New York: State University of New York Press.

Dana, Leo Paul (1996), "Albania in the Twilight Zone: The *Perseritje* Model and its Impact on Small Business," *Journal of Small Business Management,* 24 (1), January, pp. 64-70.

Dana, Leo Paul (1997a), "Change, Entrepreneurship and Innovation in the Republic of Kazakhstan," *Entrepreneurship, Innovation, and Change* 6 (2), June, pp.167-174.

Dana, Leo Paul (1997b), *Perspectives of Enterprise,* Williamstown, Canada: Education International.

Dana, Leo Paul (1998), "Waiting for Direction in the Former Yugoslav Republic of Macedonia (FYROM)," *Journal of Small Business Management* 36 (2), April, pp. 62-67.

Dana, Leo Paul (1999a), "Bulgaria at the Crossroads of Entrepreneurship," *Journal of Euromarketing* 8 (4), pp. 27-50.

Dana, Leo Paul (1999b), "Preserving Culture Through Small Business: Government Support for Artisans and Craftsmen in Greece," *Journal of Small Business Management* 37 (1), January, pp. 90-92.

Dana, Leo Paul (1999c), "Small Business in Israel," *Journal of Small Business Management* 37 (4), October, pp. 73-79.

Dana, Leo Paul (1999d), "The Social Cost of Tourism: A Case Study of Ios," *Cornell Quarterly* 40 (4), August 1999, pp. 60-63.

Dana, Leo Paul (2000a), "Change & Circumstance in Kyrgyz Markets," *Qualitative Market Research* 3 (2), April 2000, pp. 62-73.

Dana, Leo Paul (2000b), "Economic Sectors in Egypt & Their Managerial Implications," *Journal of African Business* 1 (1), January, pp. 65-81.

Dana, Leo Paul (2000c), "Turkey: Entrepreneurship at the Crossroads," in David L. Moore and Sam Fullerton, (eds.), *International Business Practices,* Ypsilanti, Michigan: The Academy of Business Administration, pp. 172-178.

Dana, Leo Paul and Teresa E. Dana (2000), "Taking Sides on the Island of Cyprus," *Journal of Small Business Management* 38 (2), April, pp. 80-87.

Dayan, Moshe (1966), *Diary of the Sinai Campaign,* London: Wiedenfield & Nicolson.

Ellis, William S., and George F. Mobley (1970), "Lebanon, Little Bible Land in the Crossfire of History," *National Geographic* 137 (2), February, pp. 240-275.

Harold, Frederick (1892), *The New Exodus,* London: C.P. Putnam's Sons.

Herzl, Theodore (1896), *The Jewish State: An Attempt to Solve the Jewish Question.*

Herzl, Théodore (1926), *L'Etat Juif: Essai d'une Solution de la Question Juive,* Paris: Lipschutz.

Jordan Times (1999), "Syrian Evaded Boycott of Israel to Import Printer," Volume 25 (7320), December 7, p. 1a.

Kibris Northern Cyprus Weekly (1997), "The Real Thing," Volume V, N° 8, September 30, p. 6.

Ladbury, Sarah (1984), "Choice, Chance or No Alternative?" in R. Ward and R. Jenkins (eds.), *Ethnic Communities in Business: Strategies for Economic Survival,* Cambridge: Cambridge University Press, pp. 89-124.

Luthans, Fred, and Laura T. Riolli (1997), "Albania and the Bora Company: Lessons Learned Before the Recent Crisis," *The Academy of Management Executive* 11 (3), August, pp. 61-72.

Mann, Peggy (1973), *Golda,* New York: Washington Square Press.

Mostert, Noel (1972), "The Real Revolution is Yet to Come," *The Montreal Star News and Review,* March 11, p. B-3.

Nasser, Gamal Abdel (1954), *The Philosophy of the Revolution,* Cairo: Ministry of National Guidance.

Proctor, Paul (2000), "Arkia Building 'Travel Factory' on Hopes of Middle East Peace," *Aviation Week & Space Technology* 152 (16), April 17, pp. 80-81.

Sayigh, Yusif A. (1962), *Entrepreneurs of Lebanon: The Role of the Business Leader in a Developing Economy*, Cambridge: Harvard.

Williams, John J., and Leo Paul Dana (forthcoming), *Business Opportunities in Israel & Egypt,* Singapore: Prentice Hall.

Index

D

E

By the Same Author …